BRODY'S

BRODY'S GHOST

BOOK 5

STORY AND ART BY
MARK CRILLEY

DARK HORSE BOOKS

President and Publisher - Mike Richardson
Digital Production - Christina McKenzie
Gray Toning Assistance - Allyson Willsey
Designer - Sandy Tanaka
Editor - Brendan Wright

Special thanks to Dave Land

Published by Dark Horse Books
A division of Dark Horse Comics, Inc.
10956 SE Main Street
Milwaukie, Oregon 97222

DarkHorse.com

To find a comic shop in your area call the Comic Shop Locator Service toll-free at (888) 266-4226
International Licensing: (503) 905-2377

First edition: April 2014
ISBN 978-1-61655-460-6

BRODY'S GHOST BOOK 5

    0 9 8 7 6 5 4 3 2 1

Printed in the United States of America

THIS BOOK IS DEDICATED
TO MY YOUTUBE VIEWERS,
WHOSE SUPPORT HAS INSPIRED ME
ON EACH AND EVERY PAGE

THE STORY SO FAR...

Brody is a young man living in a decaying metropolis a number of decades from now. After being dumped by his girlfriend Nicole, he allowed his life to spiral into a directionless mess. One afternoon he finds himself face to face with the ghost of a teenage girl, Talia, who enlists his help in pursuing a serial killer known as the Penny Murderer. After training with an ancient samurai ghost named Kagemura, Brody acquires great physical strength and, in time, powers of telekinesis and extrasensory perception. Finding the killer grows more urgent when Brody's ESP shows him that Nicole is destined to be the next victim. He then gathers clues about the Penny Murderer by posing as a police detective and interviewing the victims' families.

Brody's one ally in town is his old friend Gabe, a cop who helps him sneak into police headquarters to examine evidence related to the killings. There Brody has a series of bizarre visions that come straight from the Penny Murderer's brain, among them that of a lamb, which Gabe later suggests may be the killer's preferred symbol of innocence. It all goes off the rails when Brody is antagonized by Nicole's new boyfriend Landon, a hotshot in the finance world with connections to both the mob and the police. Landon has his thugs trash Brody's apartment, and the all-out confrontation that ensues between the two of them ends in Brody sending Landon through one of the windows of his own house. At that very moment, Nicole arrives at the scene, and—thinking that Brody has gone crazy and attacked Landon for no good reason—calls the police.

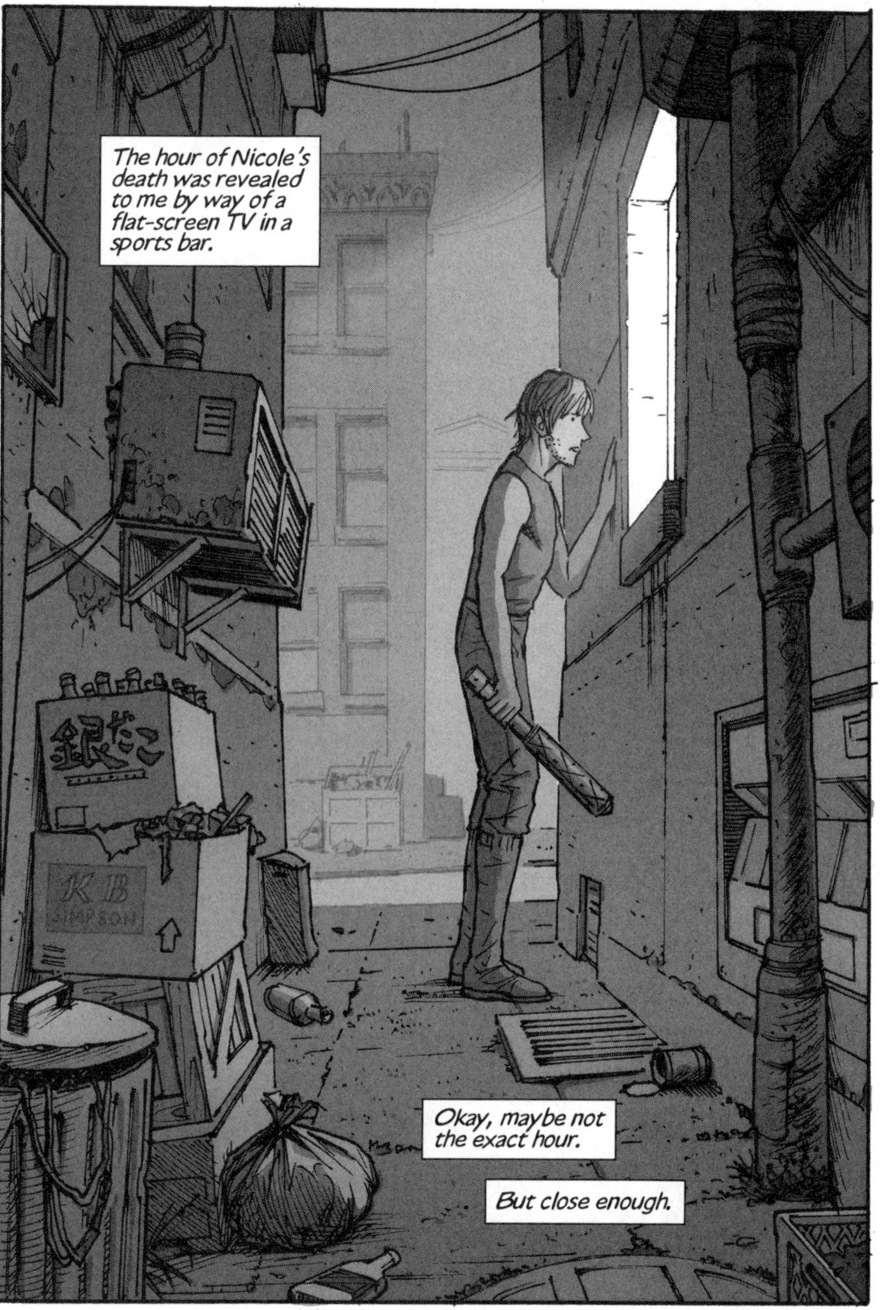
The hour of Nicole's death was revealed to me by way of a flat-screen TV in a sports bar.
銀だこ
KB
SIMPSON
Okay, maybe not the exact hour.
But close enough.

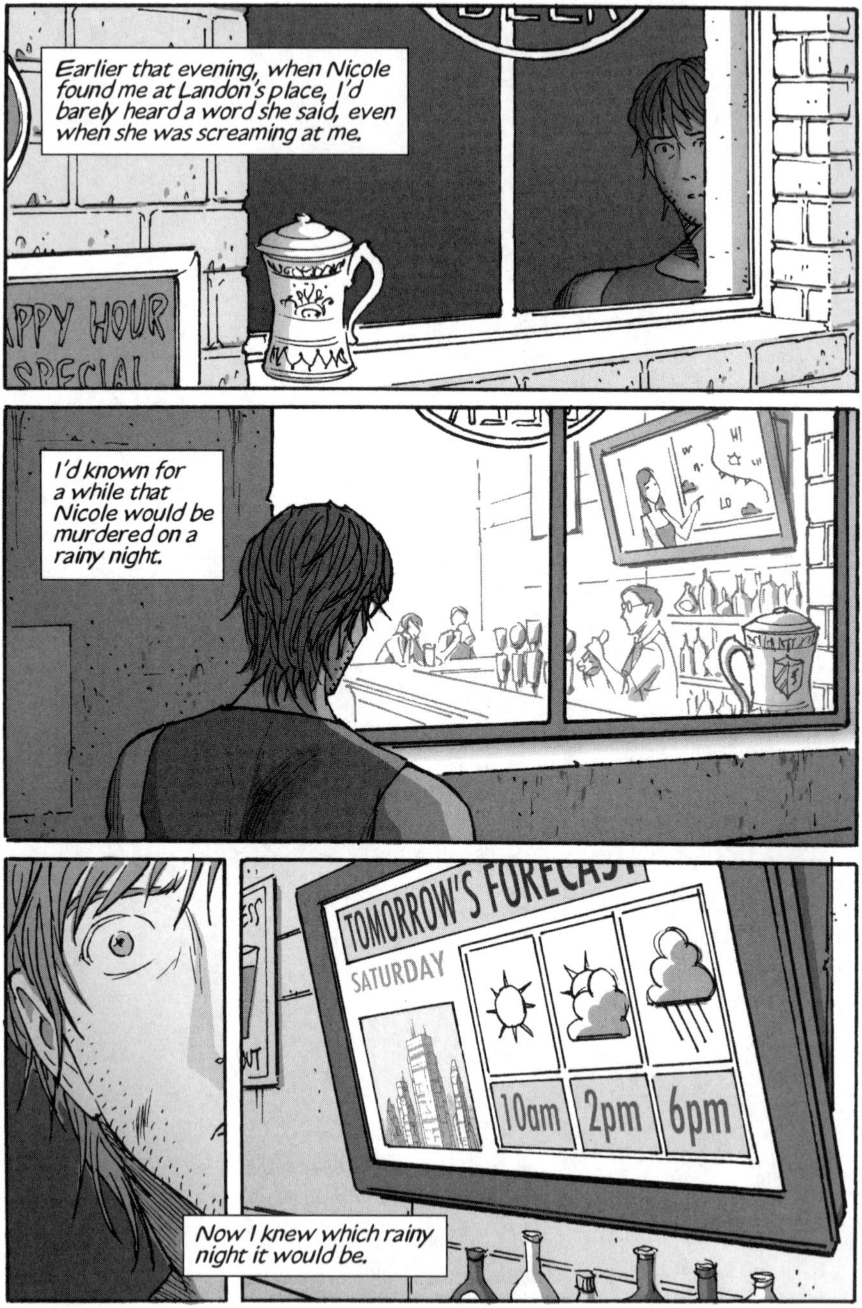
Earlier that evening, when Nicole found me at Landon's place, I'd barely heard a word she said, even when she was screaming at me.
PPY HOUR
I'd known for a while that Nicole would be murdered on a rainy night.
HI
LO
TOMORROW'S FORECAS
SATURDAY
10am
2pm
6pm
Now I knew which rainy night it would be.

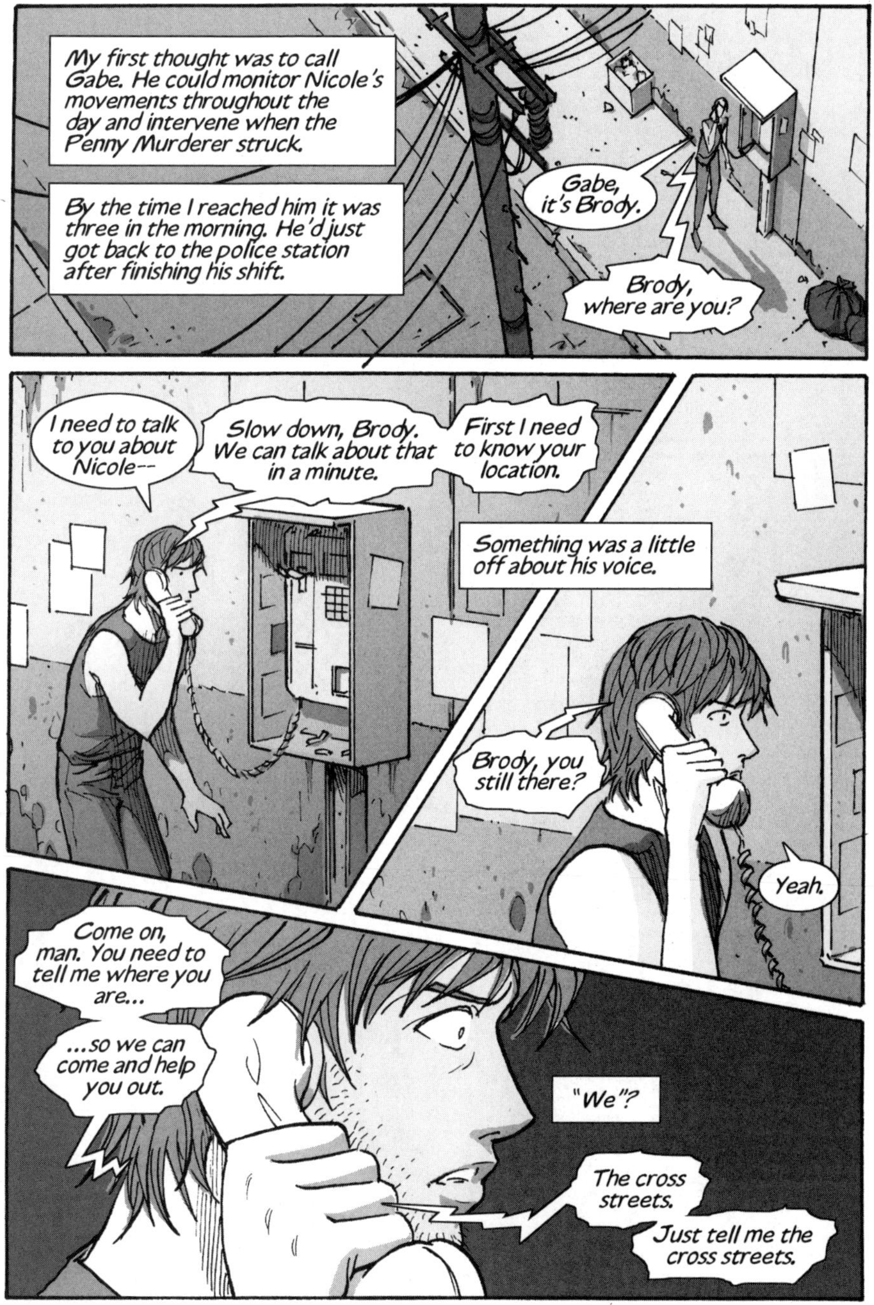
My first thought was to call Gabe. He could monitor Nicole's movements throughout the day and intervene when the Penny Murderer struck.
By the time I reached him it was three in the morning. He'd just got back to the police station after finishing his shift.
Gabe, it's Brody.
Brody, where are you?
I need to talk to you about Nicole--
Slow down, Brody. We can talk about that in a minute.
First I need to know your location.
Something was a little off about his voice.
Brody, you still there?
Yeah.
Come on, man. You need to tell me where you are...
...so we can come and help you out.
"We"?
The cross streets.
Just tell me the cross streets.

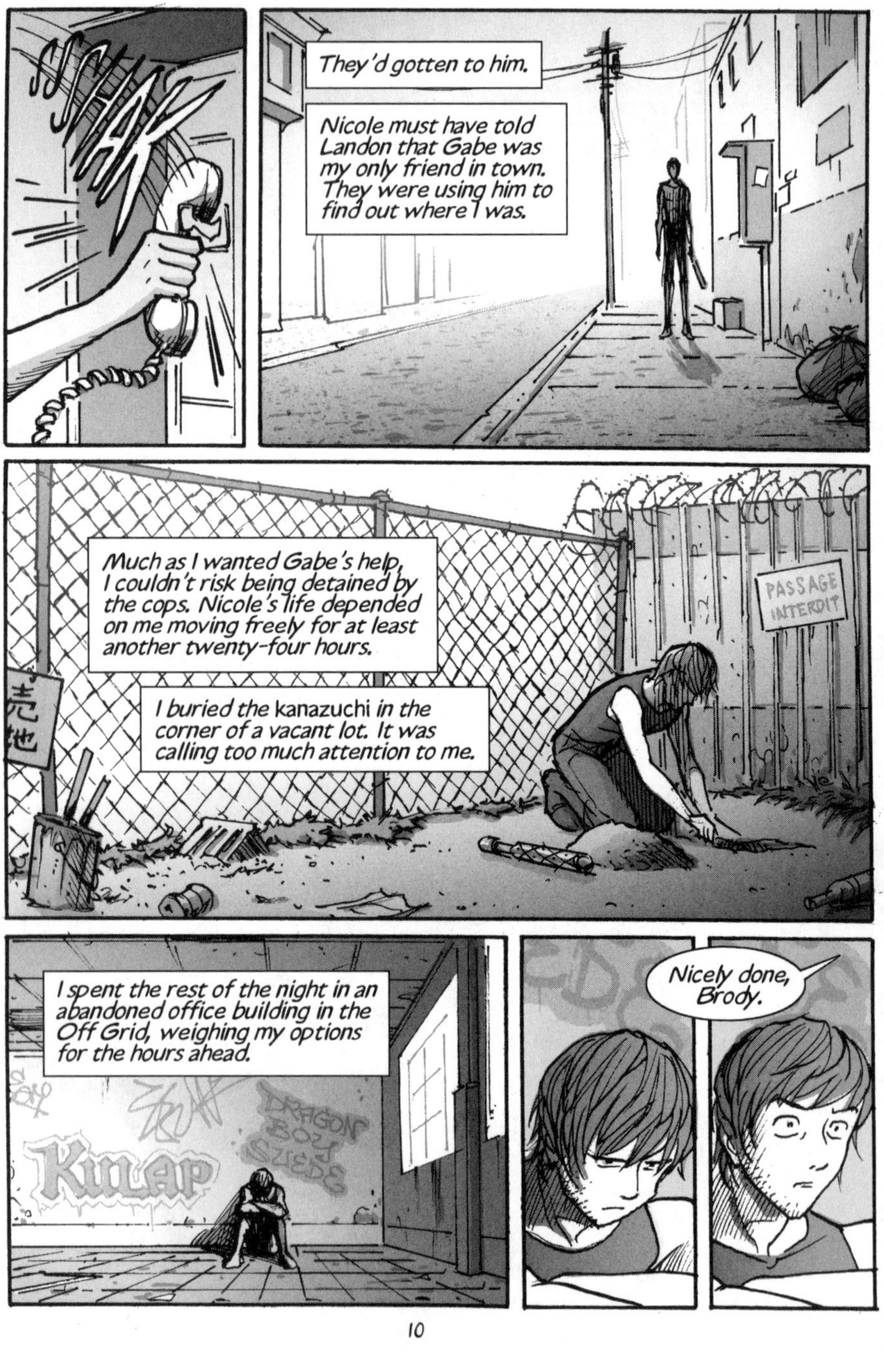
SSSHAK
They'd gotten to him.
Nicole must have told Landon that Gabe was my only friend in town. They were using him to find out where I was.
Much as I wanted Gabe's help, I couldn't risk being detained by the cops. Nicole's life depended on me moving freely for at least another twenty-four hours.
PASSAGE INTERDIT
売地
I buried the kanazuchi in the corner of a vacant lot. It was calling too much attention to me.
I spent the rest of the night in an abandoned office building in the Off Grid, weighing my options for the hours ahead.
KULAP
Nicely done, Brody.

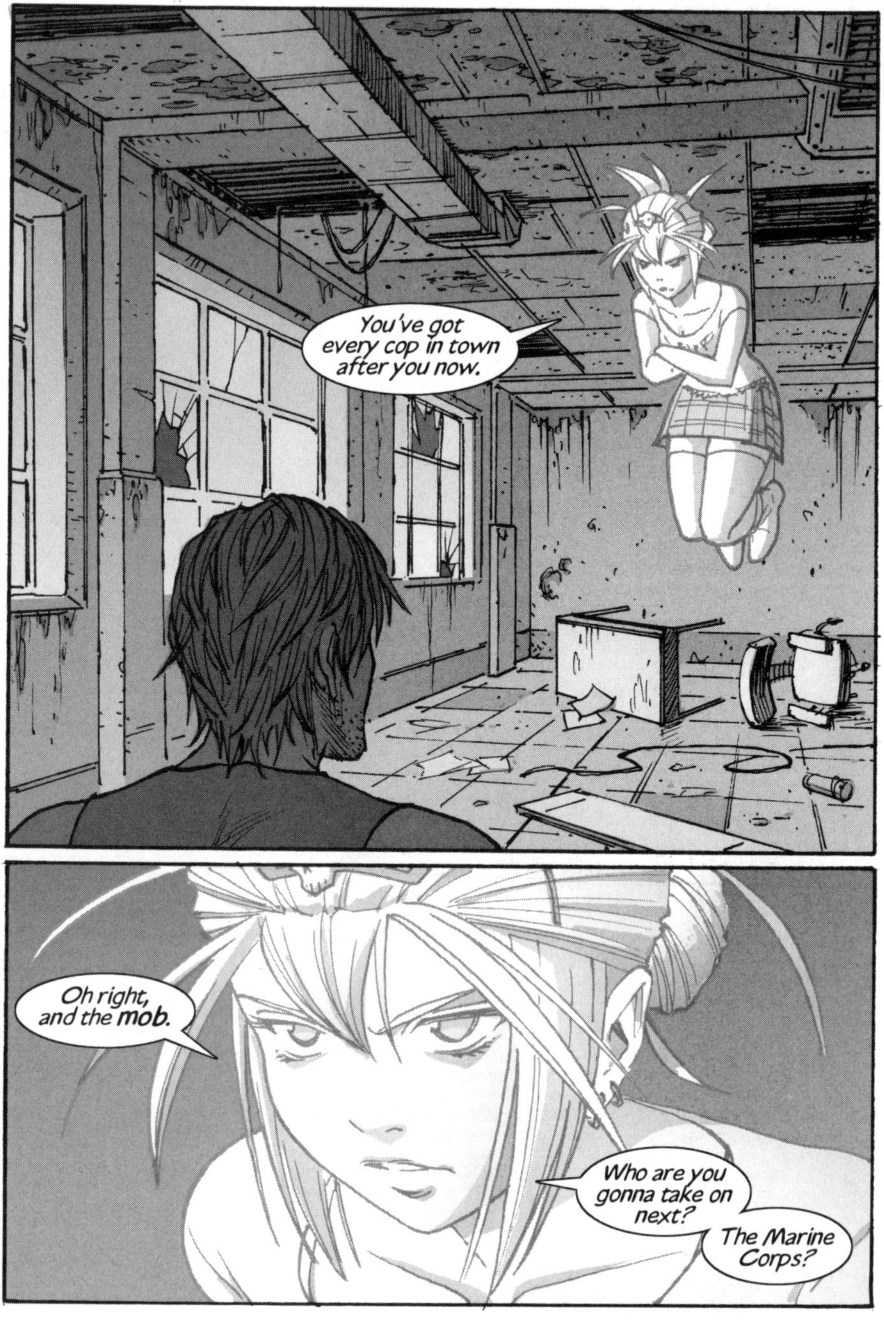
You've got every cop in town after you now.
Oh right, and the **mob**.
Who are you gonna take on next?
The Marine Corps?

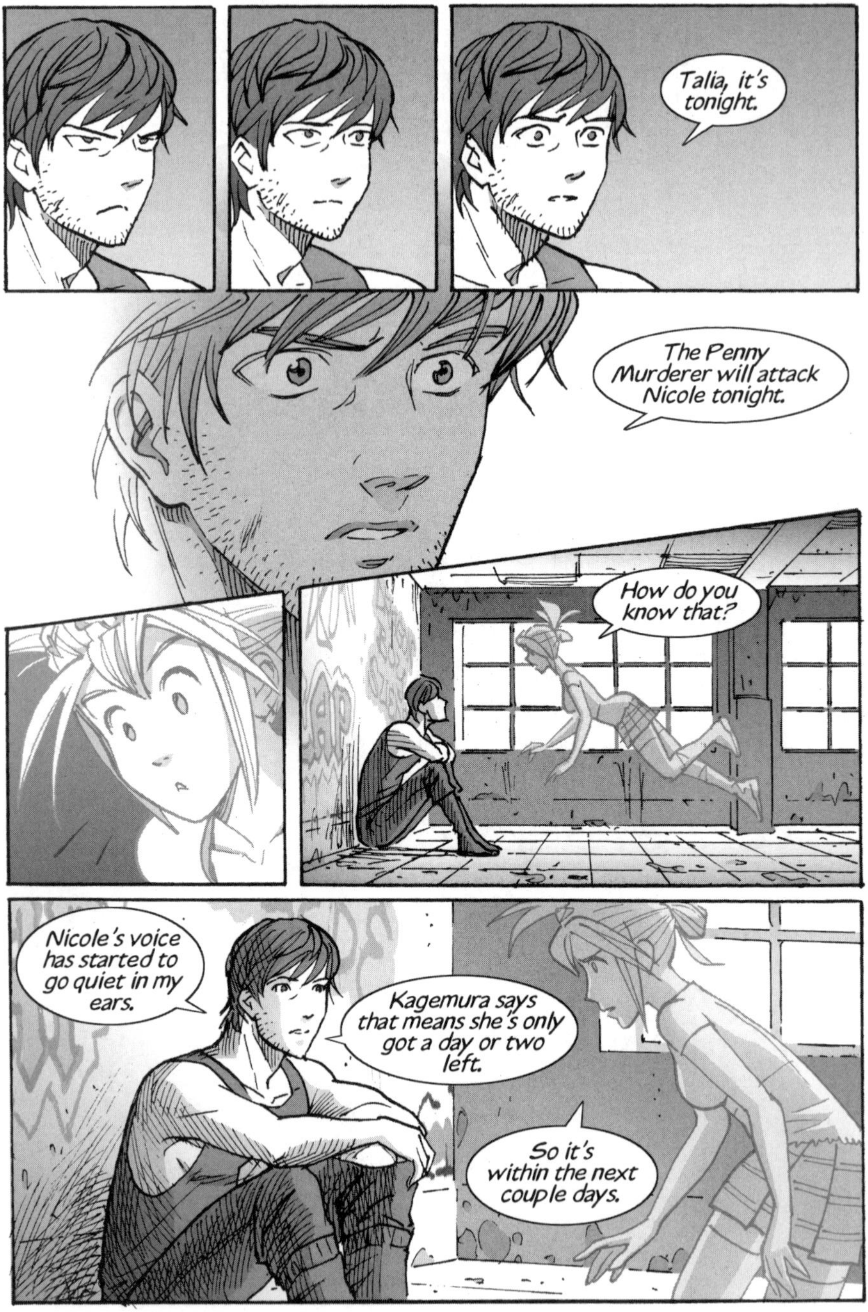
Talia, it's tonight.
The Penny Murderer will attack Nicole tonight.
How do you know that?
Nicole's voice has started to go quiet in my ears.
Kagemura says that means she's only got a day or two left.
So it's within the next couple days.

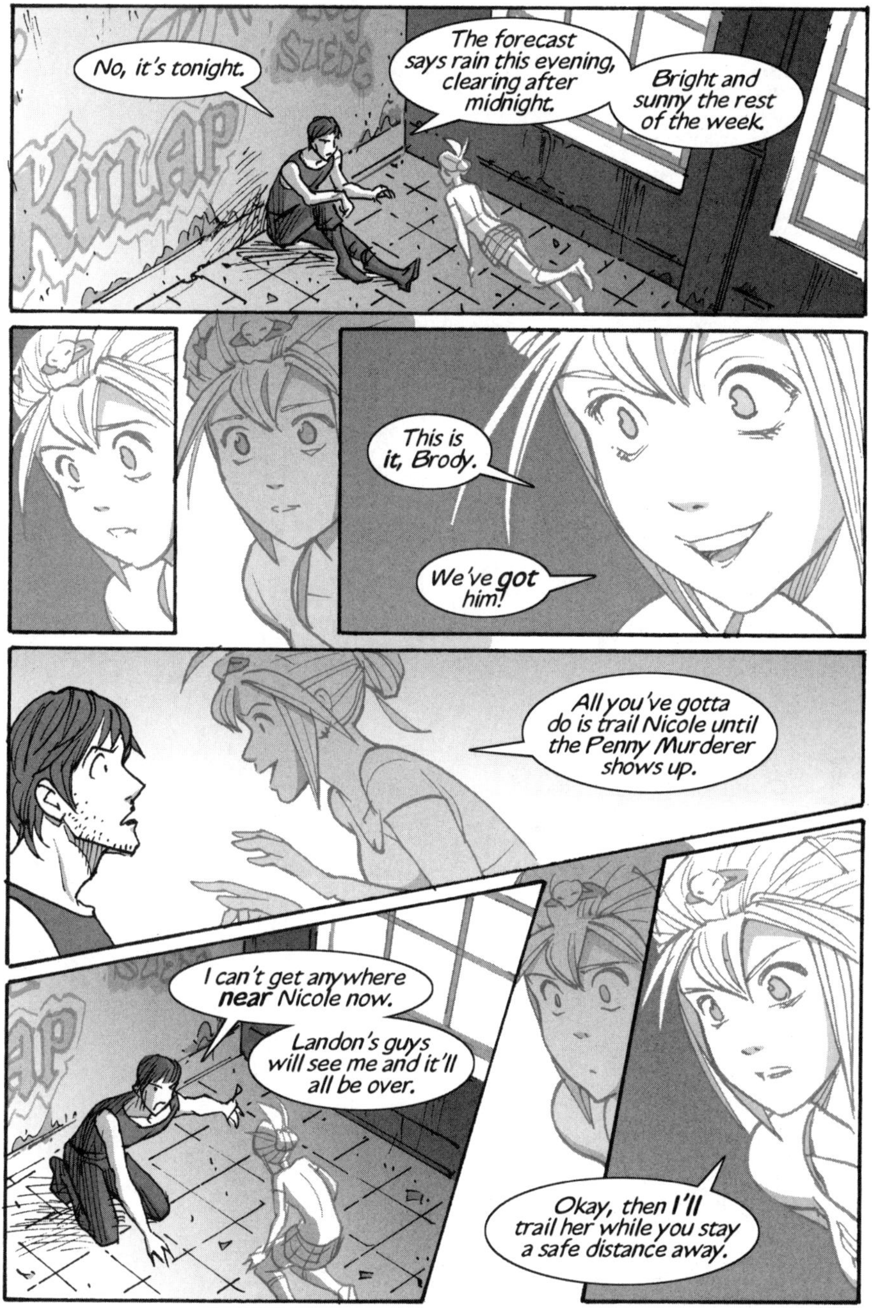
No, it's tonight.
The forecast says rain this evening, clearing after midnight.
Bright and sunny the rest of the week.
This is it, Brody.
We've got him!
All you've gotta do is trail Nicole until the Penny Murderer shows up.
I can't get anywhere near Nicole now.
Landon's guys will see me and it'll all be over.
Okay, then I'll trail her while you stay a safe distance away.

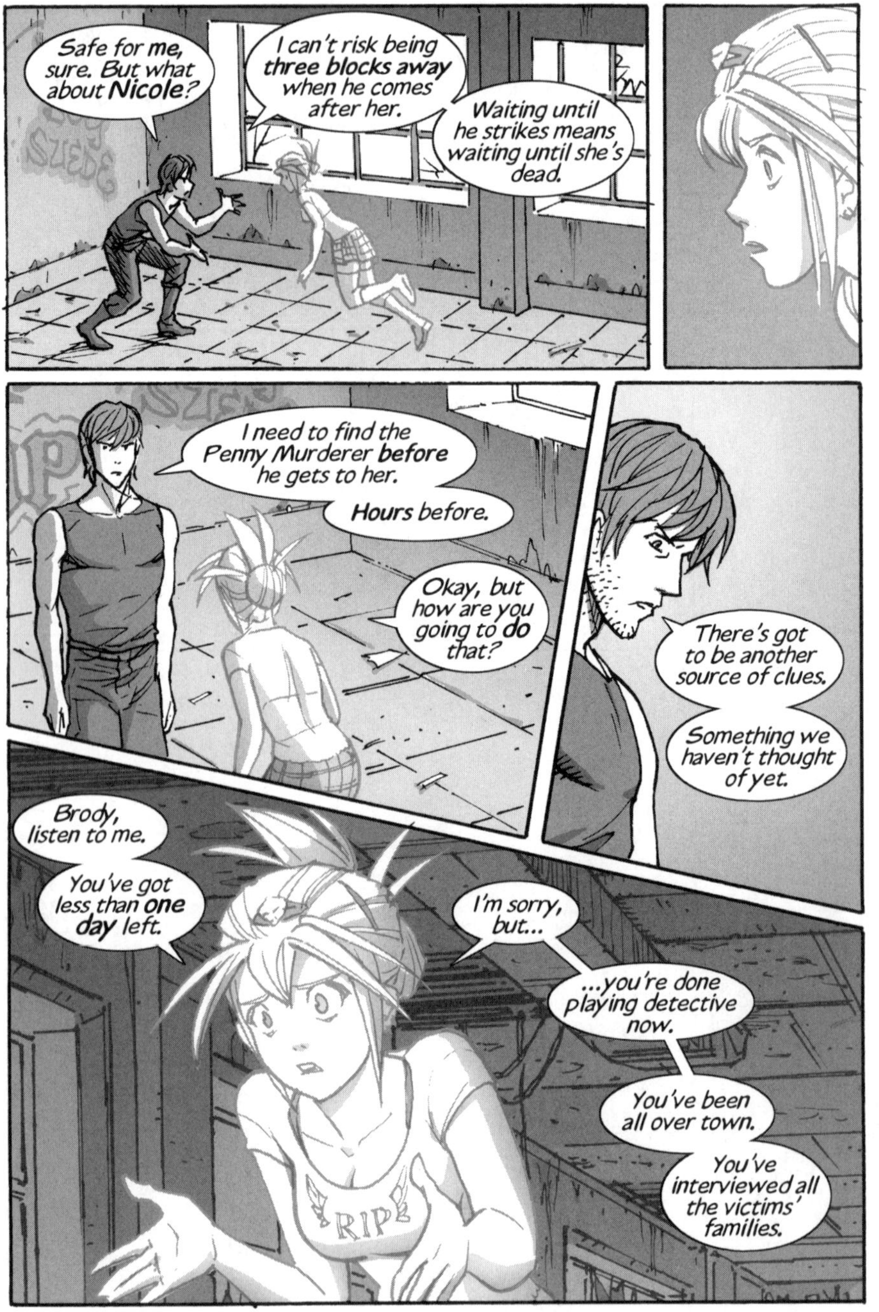
Safe for **me**, sure. But what about **Nicole**?
I can't risk being **three blocks away** when he comes after her.
Waiting until he strikes means waiting until she's dead.
I need to find the Penny Murderer **before** he gets to her.
Hours before.
Okay, but how are you going to **do** that?
There's got to be another source of clues.
Something we haven't thought of yet.
Brody, listen to me.
You've got less than **one day** left.
I'm sorry, but...
...you're done playing detective now.
You've been all over town.
You've interviewed all the victims' families.

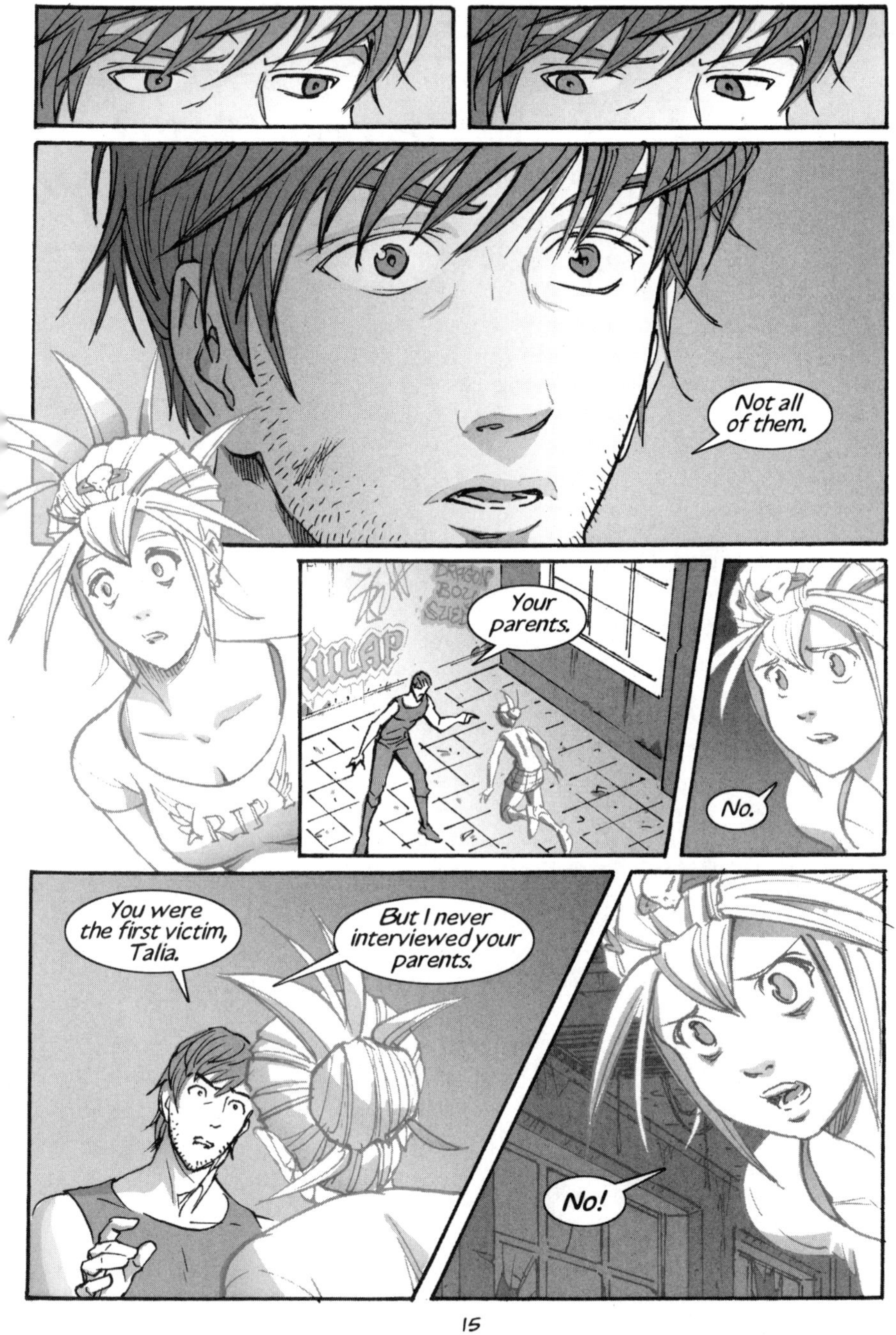
Not all of them.
Your parents.
No.
You were the first victim, Talia.
But I never interviewed your parents.
No!

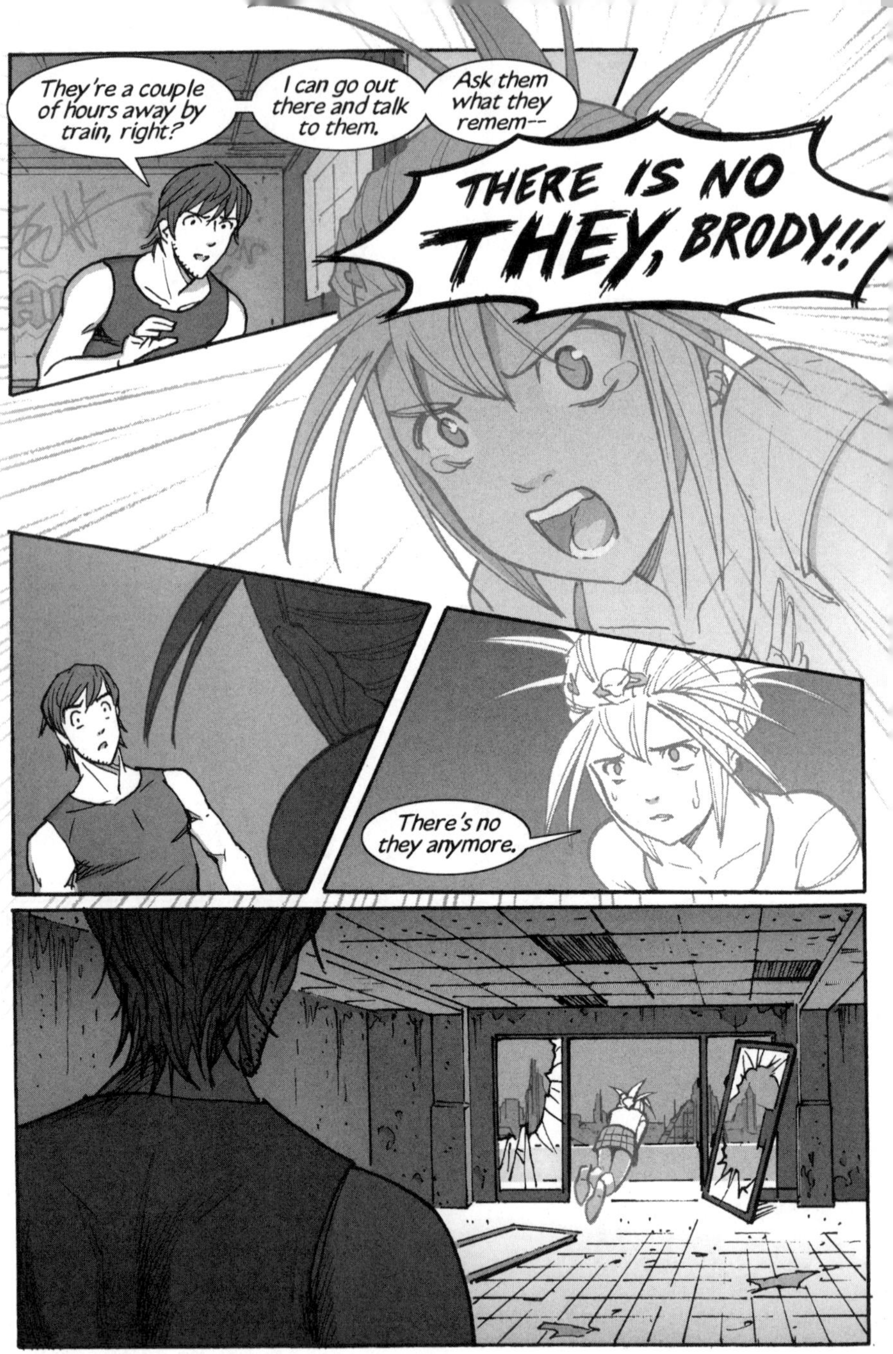
They're a couple of hours away by train, right?
I can go out there and talk to them.
Ask them what they remem--
THERE IS NO THEY, BRODY!!
There's no they anymore.

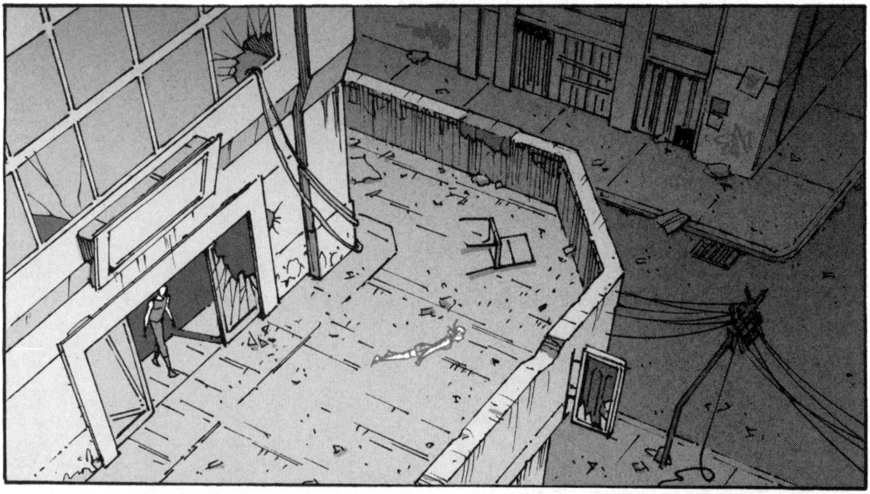

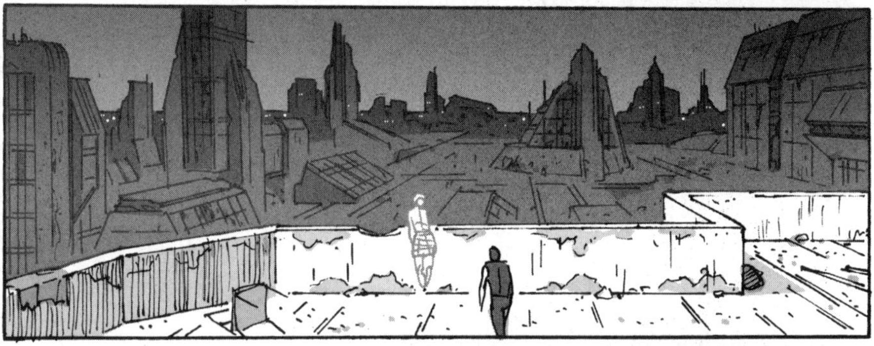

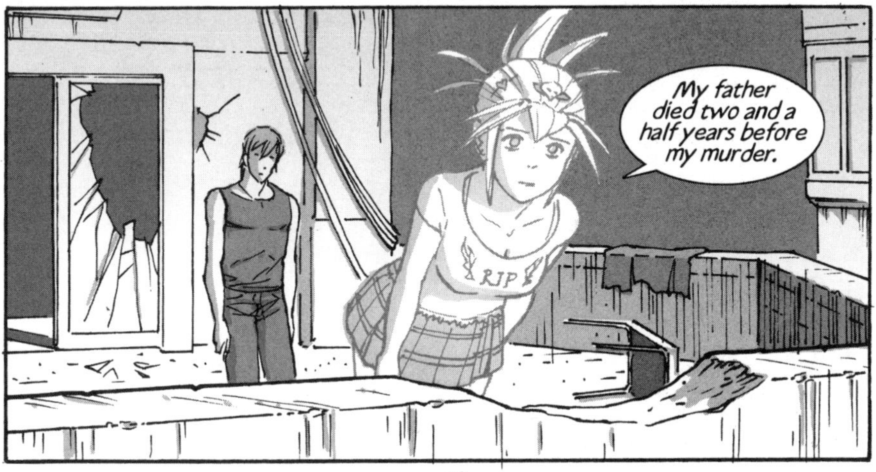
My father died two and a half years before my murder.

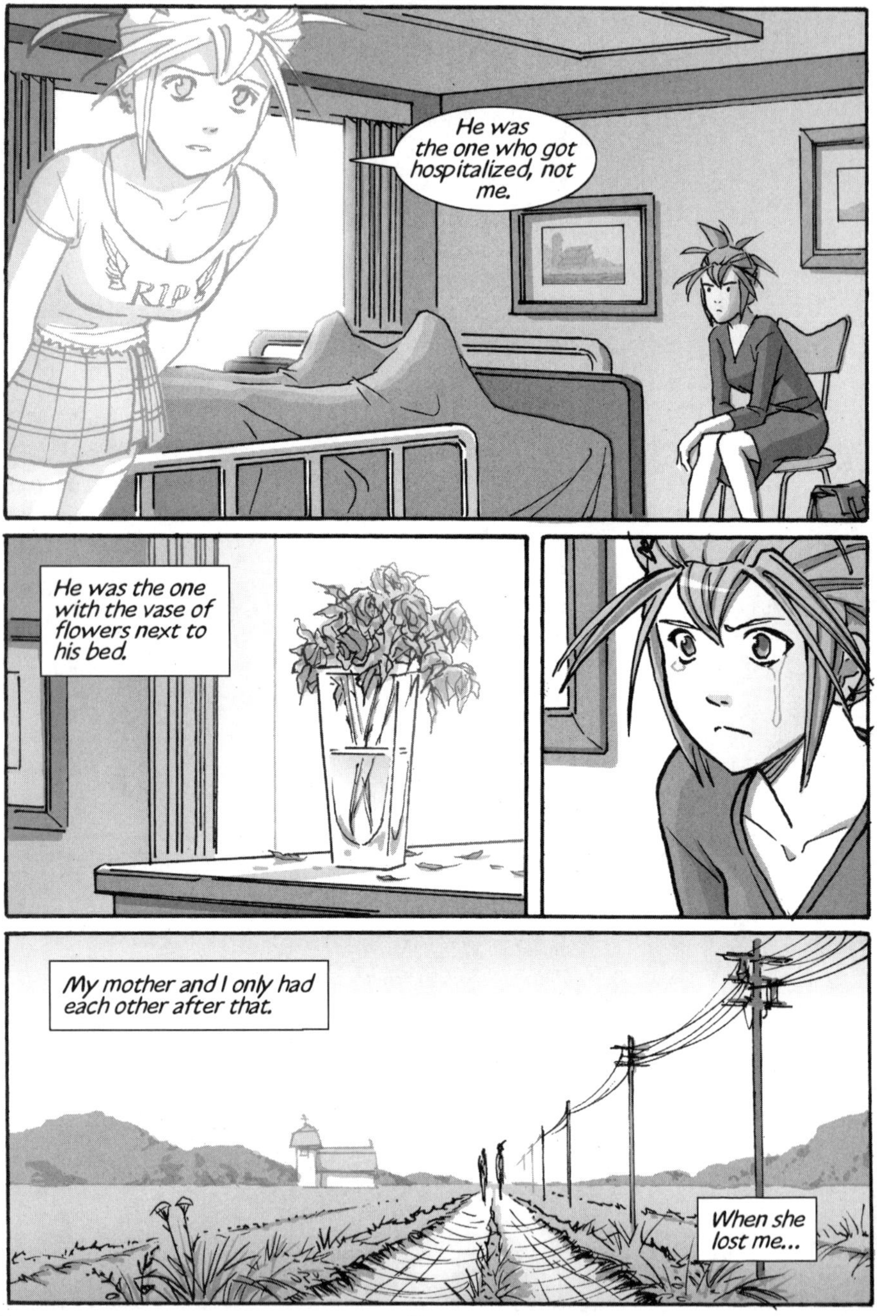

He was the one who got hospitalized, not me.
RIP
He was the one with the vase of flowers next to his bed.
My mother and I only had each other after that.
When she lost me...

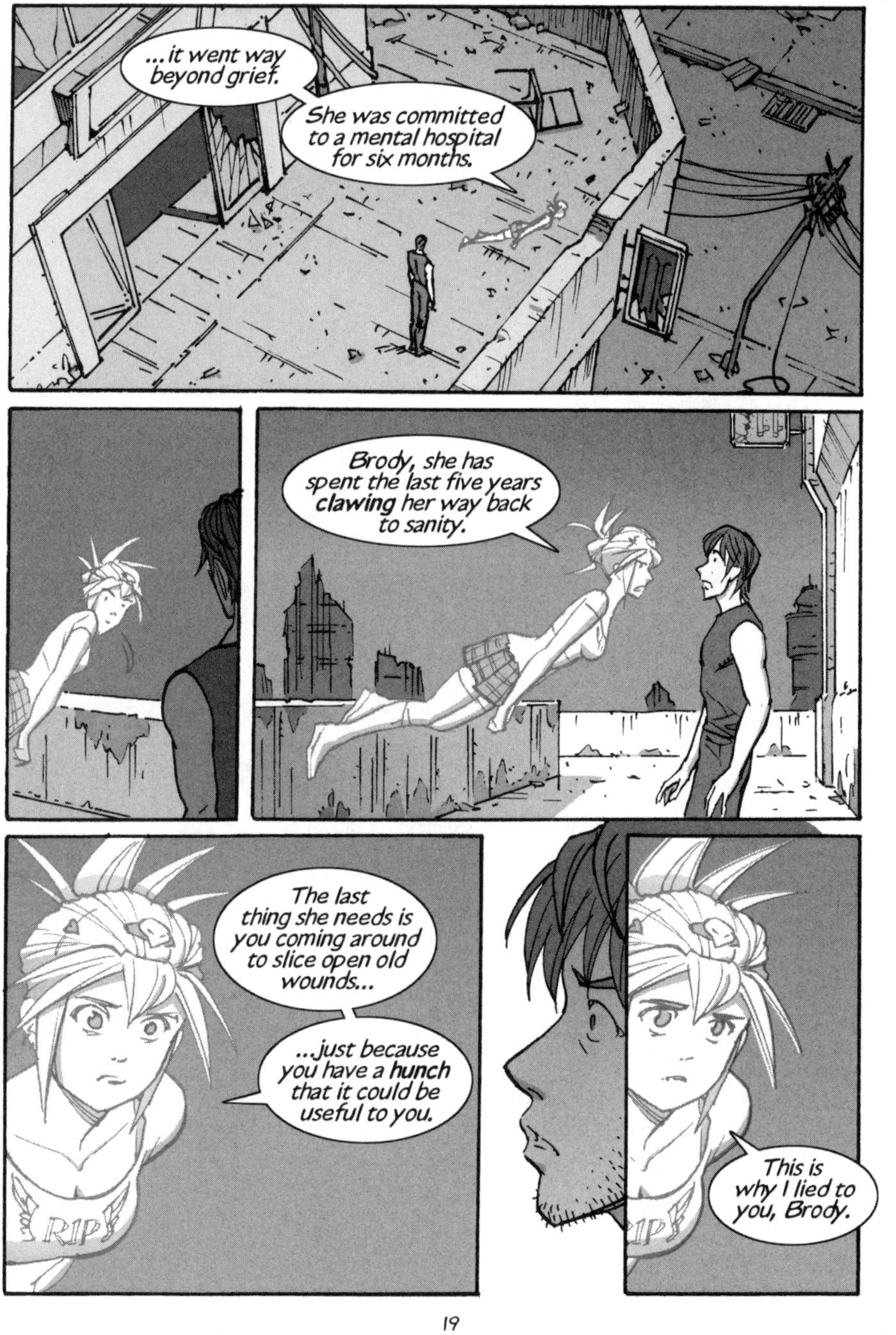
...it went way beyond grief.
She was committed to a mental hospital for six months.
Brody, she has spent the last five years **clawing** her way back to sanity.
The last thing she needs is you coming around to slice open old wounds...
...just because you have a **hunch** that it could be useful to you.
This is why I lied to you, Brody.

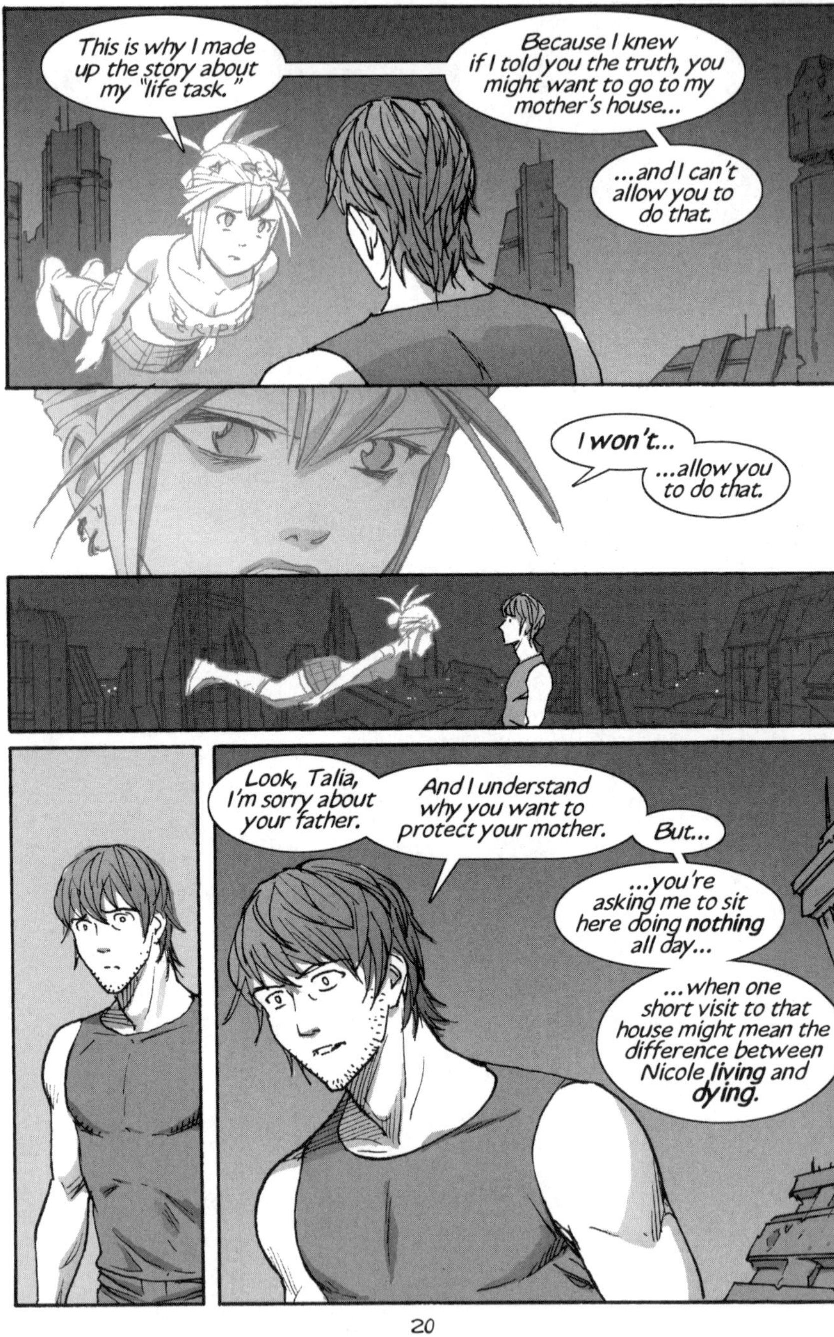
This is why I made up the story about my "life task."
Because I knew if I told you the truth, you might want to go to my mother's house...
...and I can't allow you to do that.
I **won't**...
...allow you to do that.
Look, Talia, I'm sorry about your father.
And I understand why you want to protect your mother.
But...
...you're asking me to sit here doing **nothing** all day...
...when one short visit to that house might mean the difference between Nicole **living** and **dying.**

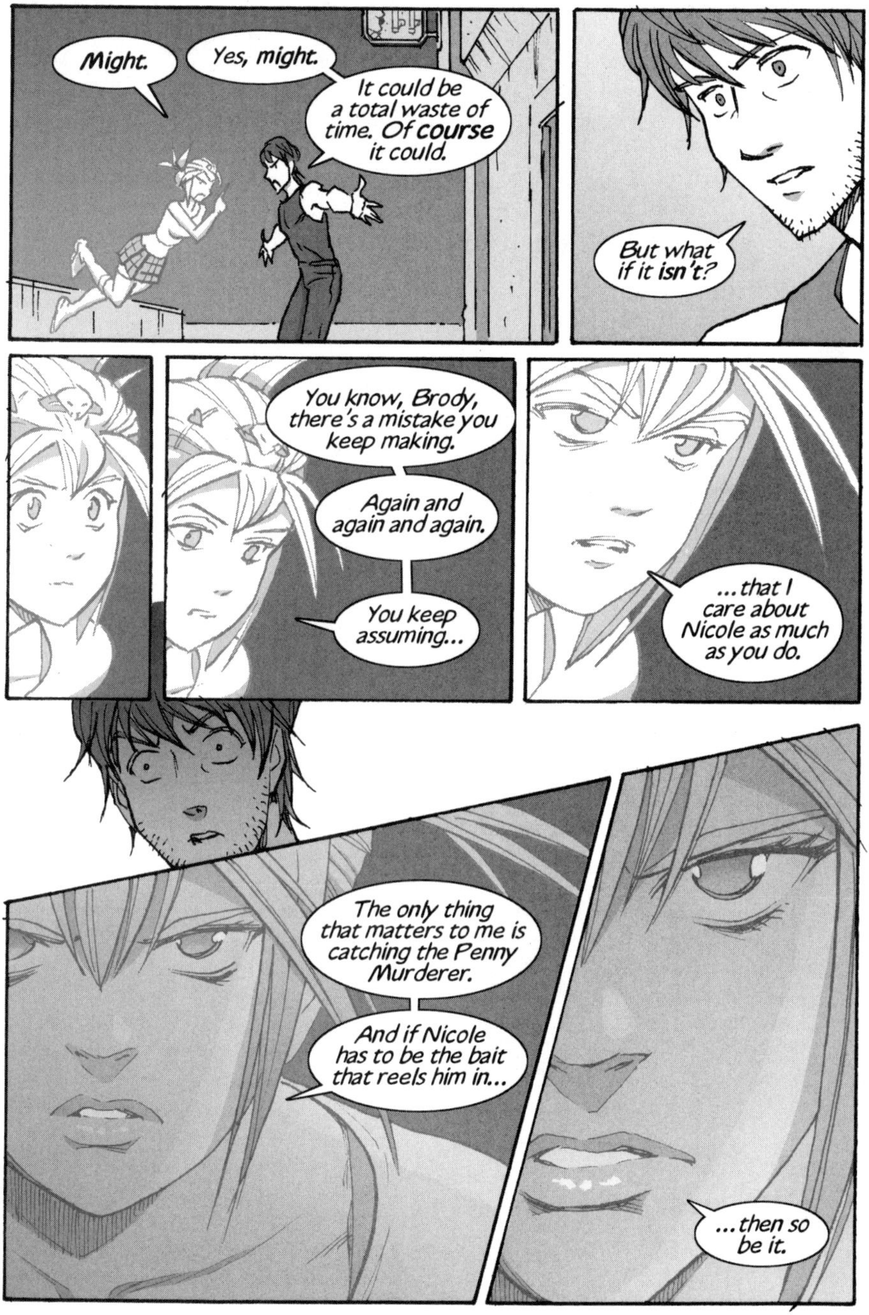
Might.
Yes, might.
It could be a total waste of time. Of course it could.
But what if it isn't?
You know, Brody, there's a mistake you keep making.
Again and again and again.
You keep assuming...
...that I care about Nicole as much as you do.
The only thing that matters to me is catching the Penny Murderer.
And if Nicole has to be the bait that reels him in...
...then so be it.

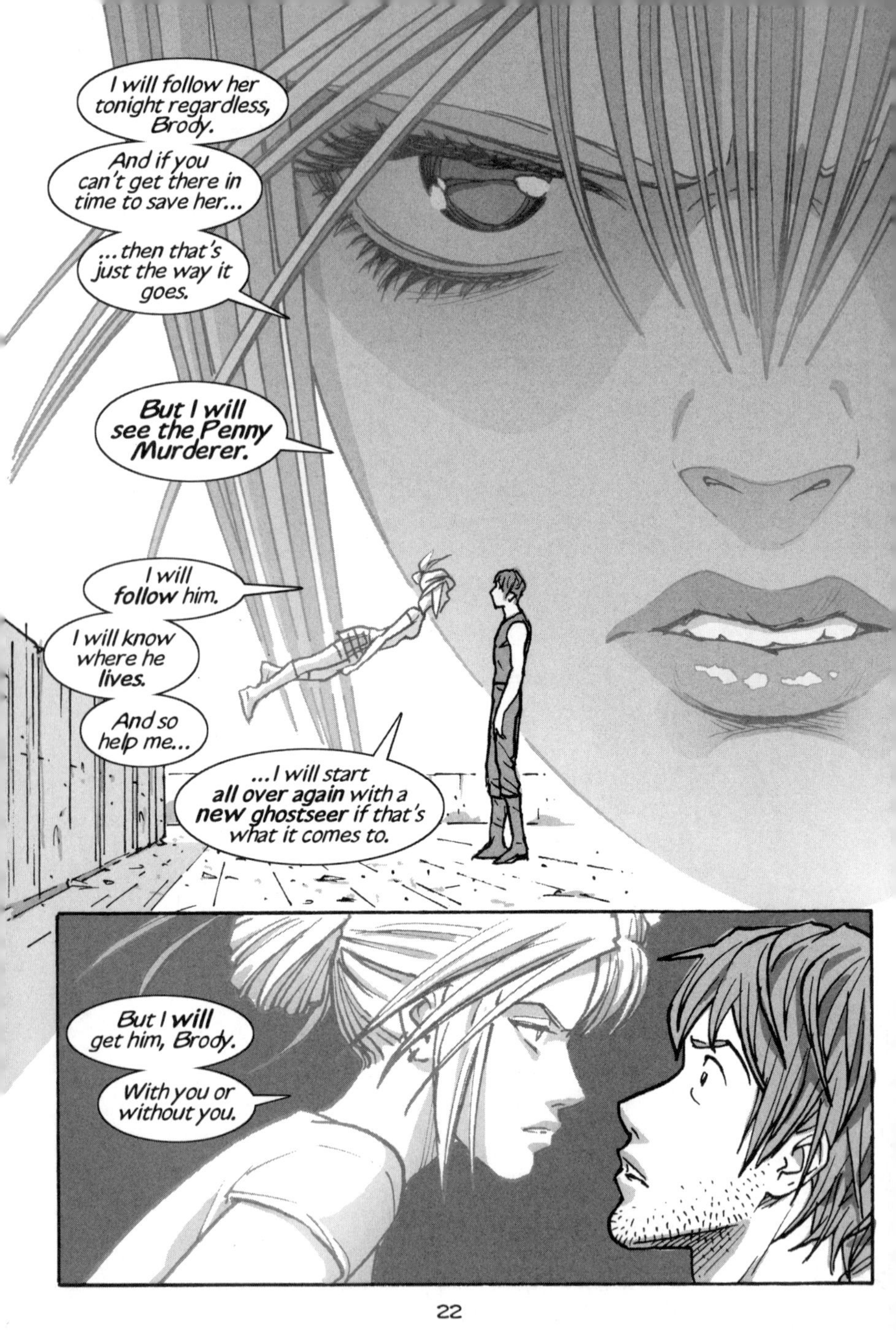
I will follow her tonight regardless, Brody.
And if you can't get there in time to save her...
...then that's just the way it goes.
But I will see the Penny Murderer.
I will follow him.
I will know where he lives.
And so help me...
...I will start all over again with a new ghostseer if that's what it comes to.
But I will get him, Brody.
With you or without you.

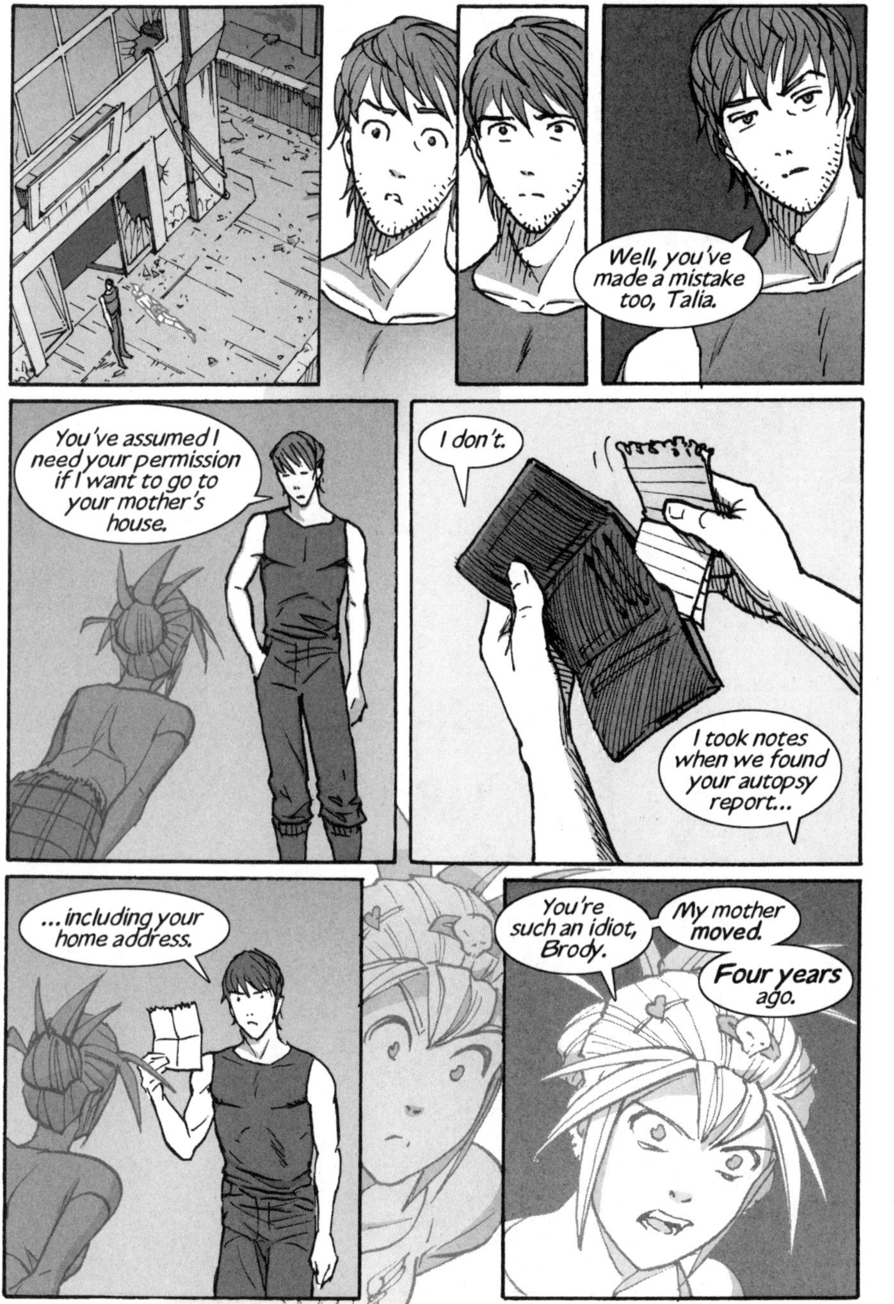
Well, you've made a mistake too, Talia.
You've assumed I need your permission if I want to go to your mother's house.
I don't.
I took notes when we found your autopsy report...
...including your home address.
You're such an idiot, Brody.
My mother moved.
Four years ago.

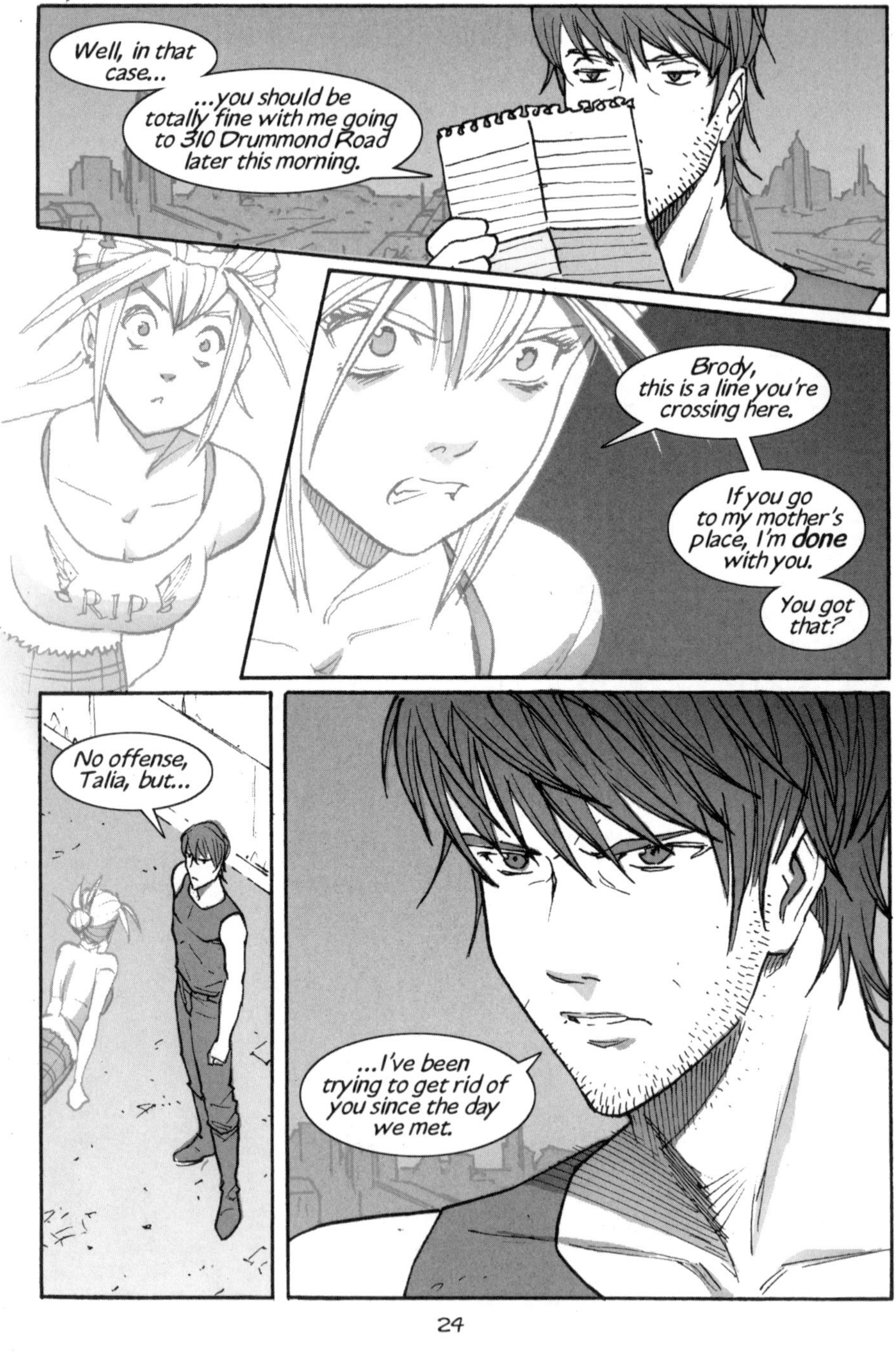
Well, in that case...
...you should be totally fine with me going to 310 Drummond Road later this morning.
Brody, this is a line you're crossing here.
If you go to my mother's place, I'm **done** with you.
You got that?
RIP
No offense, Talia, but...
...I've been trying to get rid of you since the day we met.

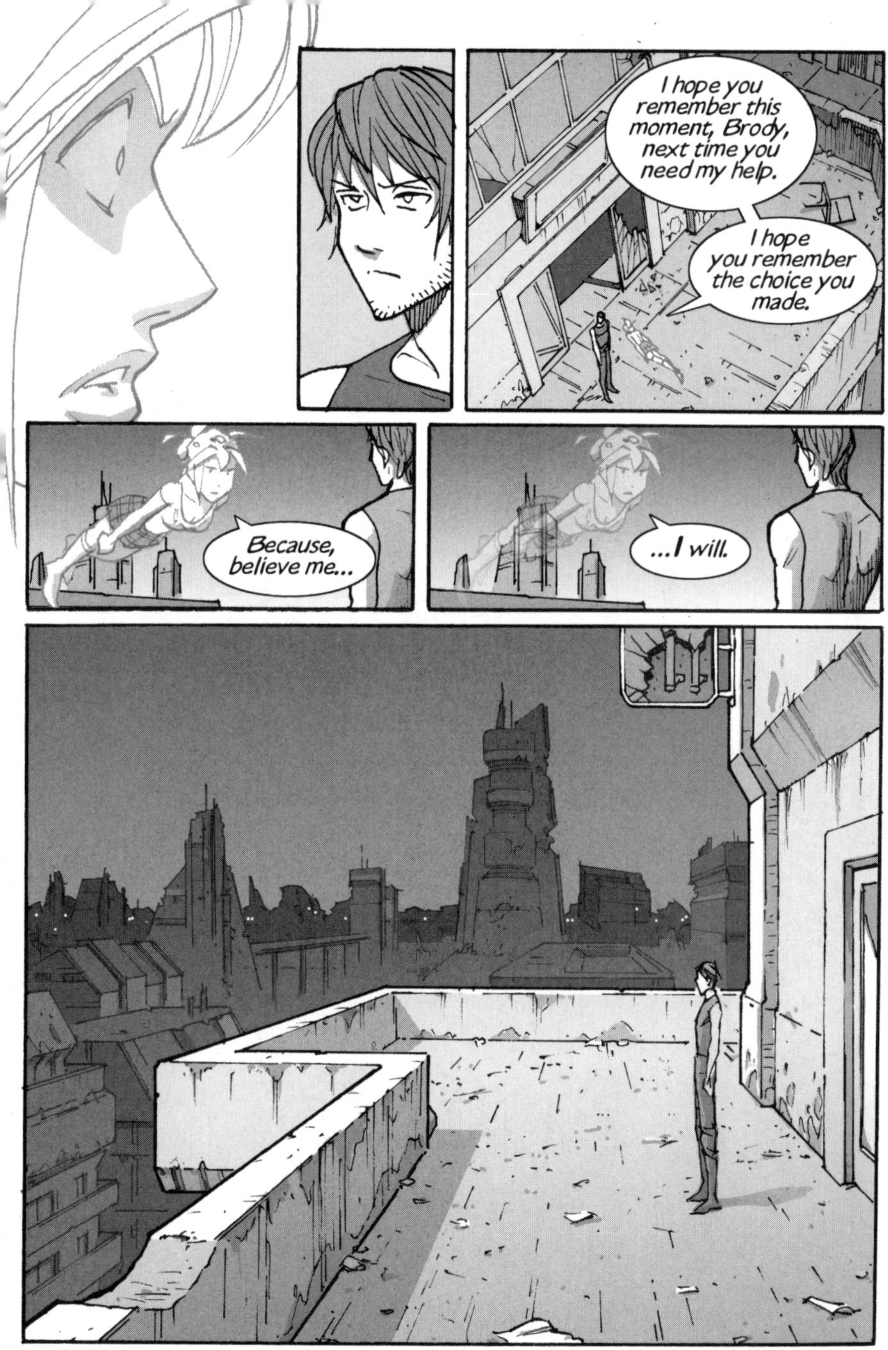
I hope you remember this moment, Brody, next time you need my help.
I hope you remember the choice you made.
Because, believe me...
...I will.

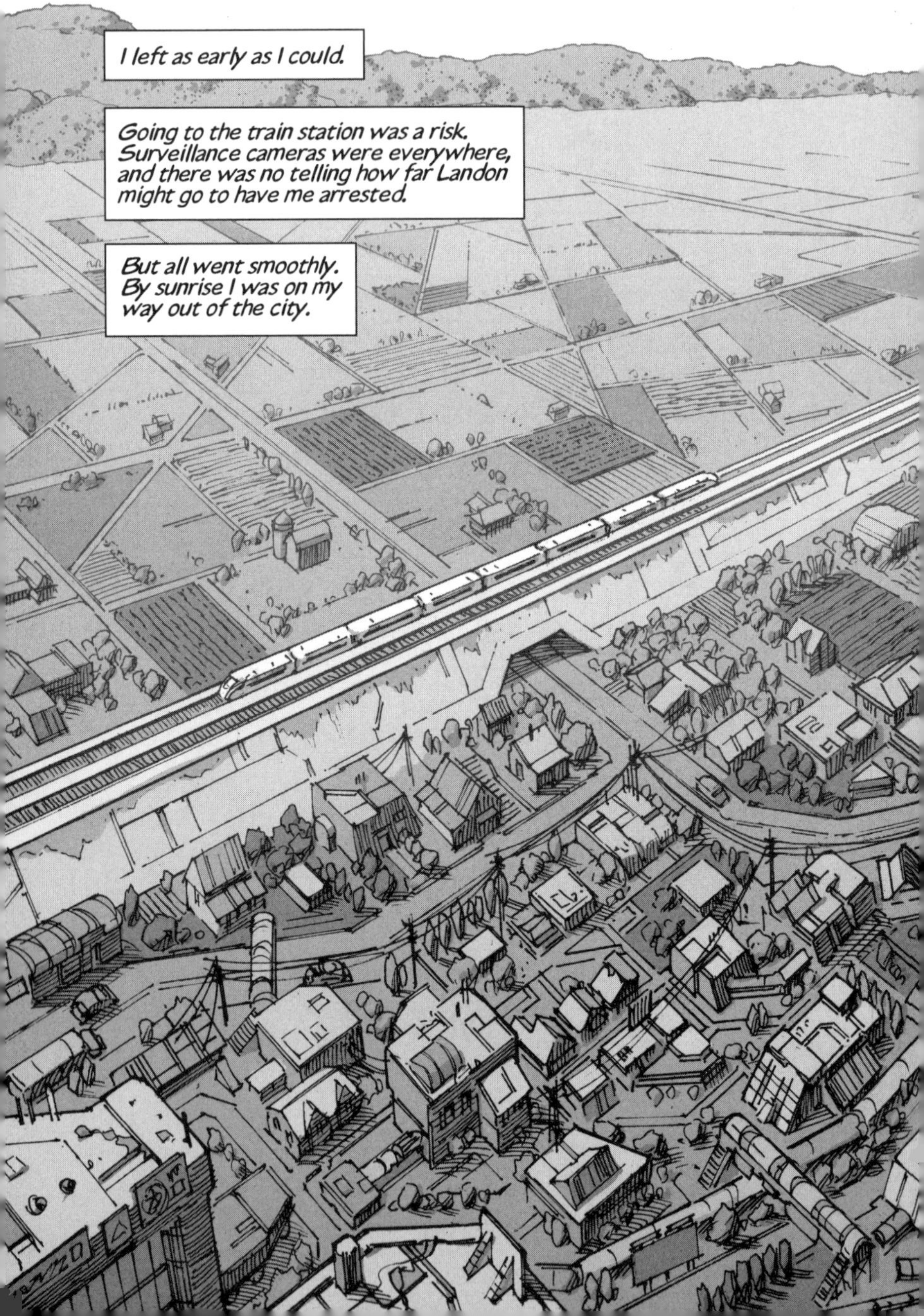
I left as early as I could.
Going to the train station was a risk. Surveillance cameras were everywhere, and there was no telling how far Landon might go to have me arrested.
But all went smoothly. By sunrise I was on my way out of the city.

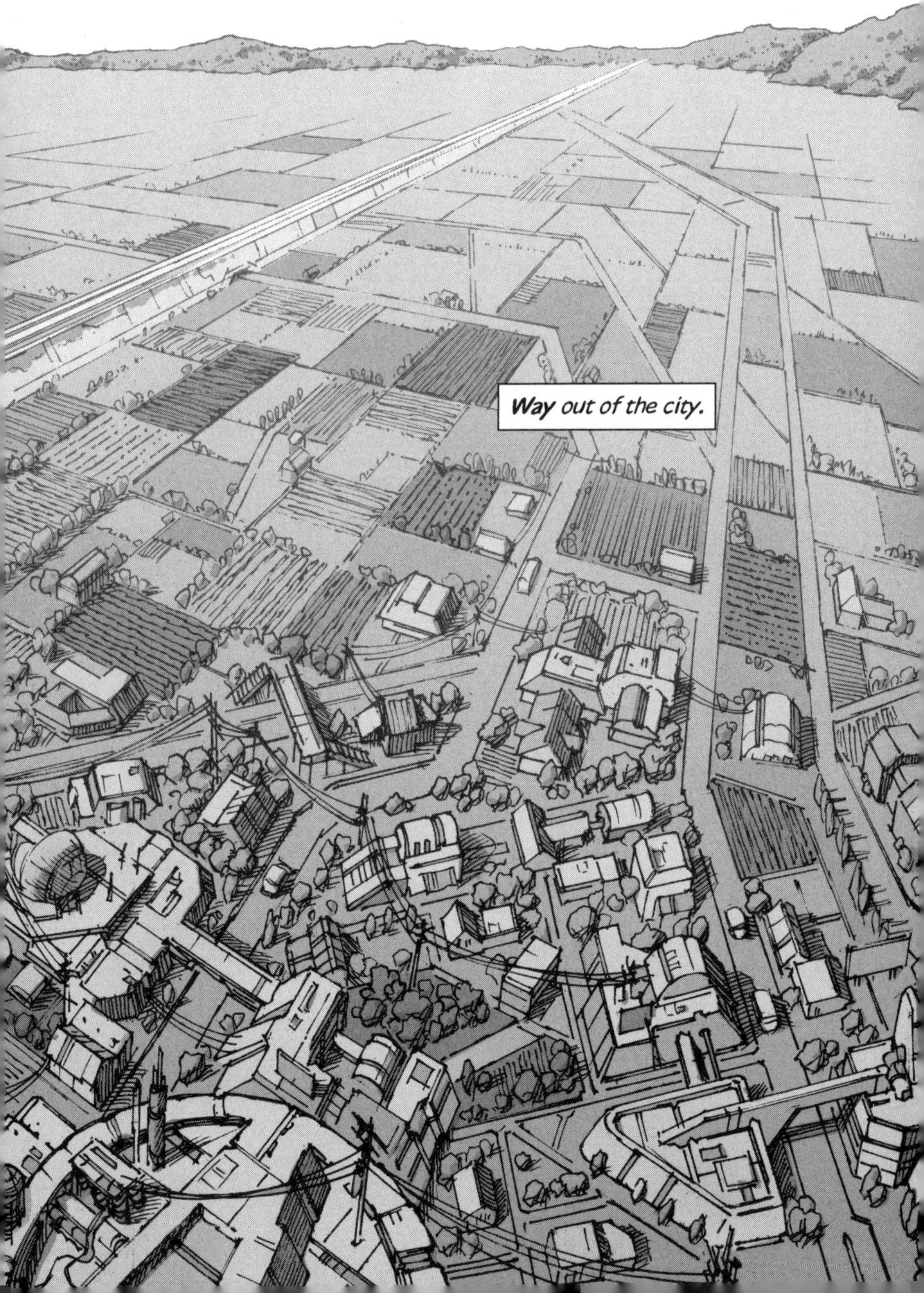
Way out of the city.

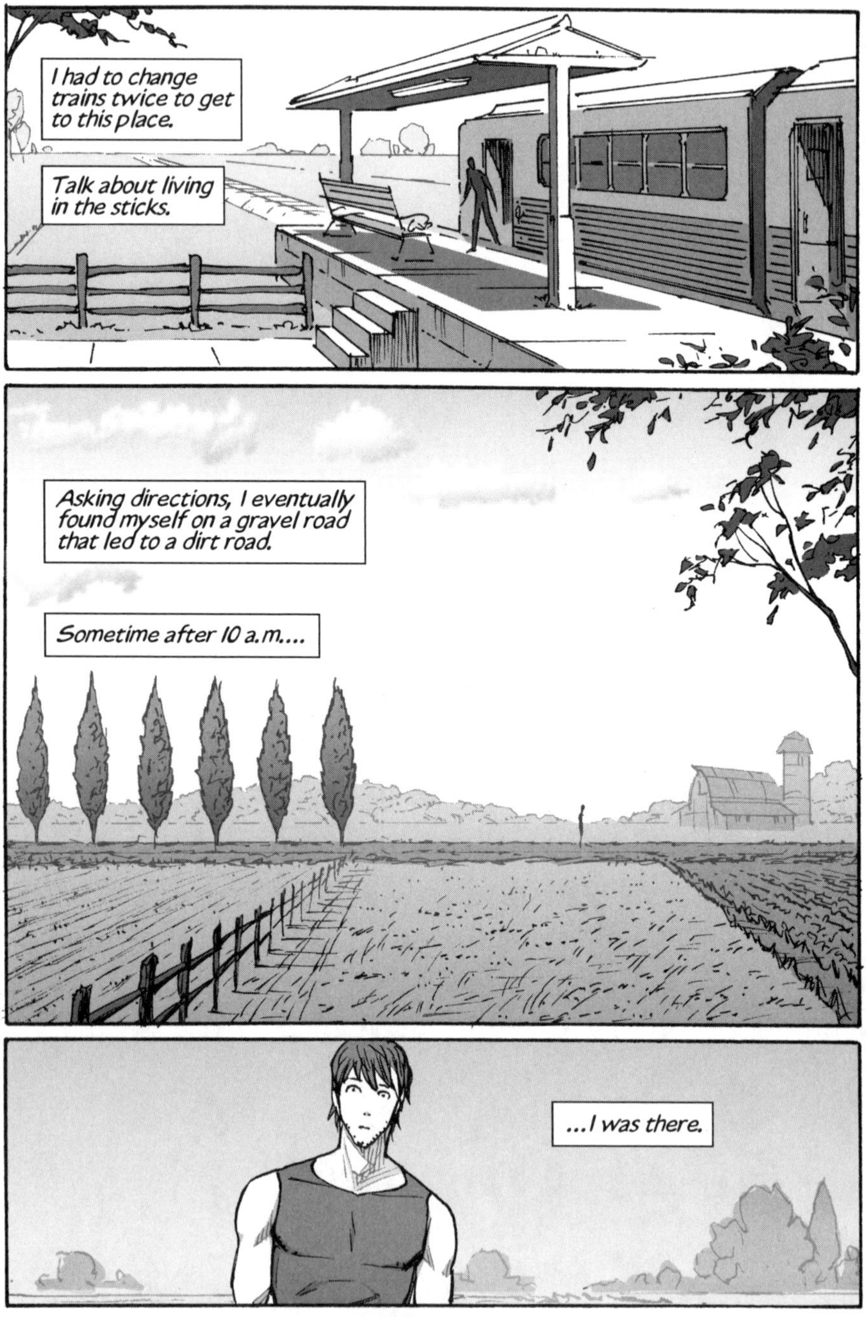
I had to change trains twice to get to this place.
Talk about living in the sticks.
Asking directions, I eventually found myself on a gravel road that led to a dirt road.
Sometime after 10 a.m....
...I was there.

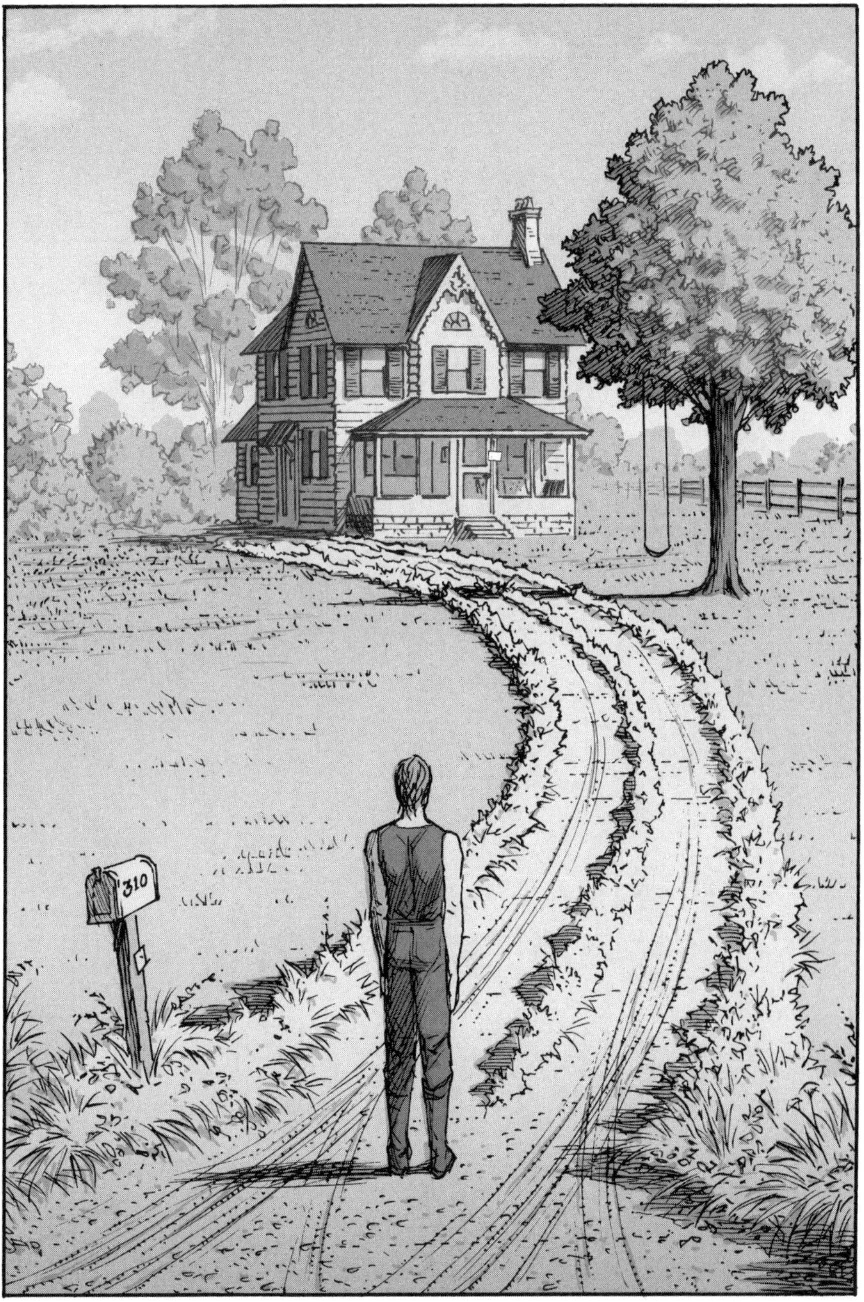
310

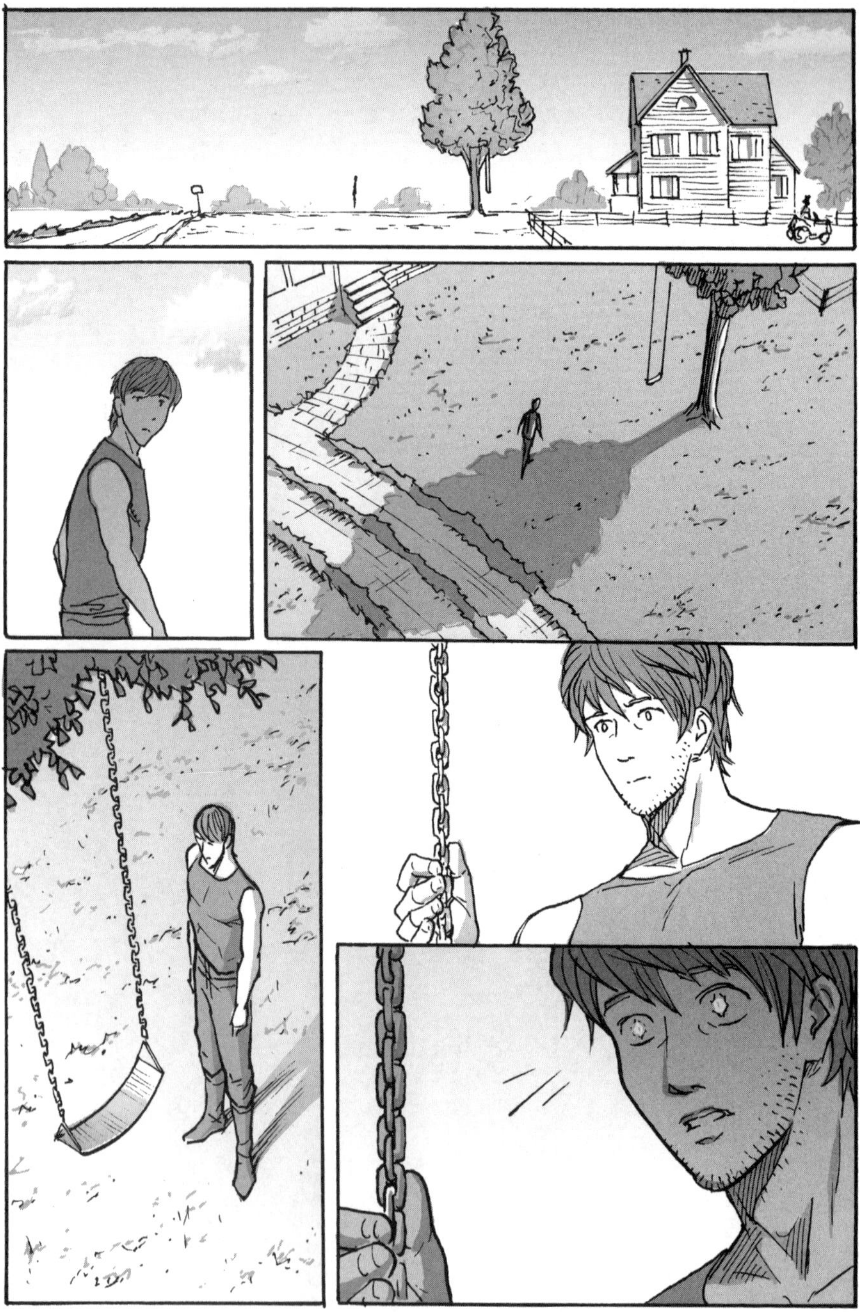

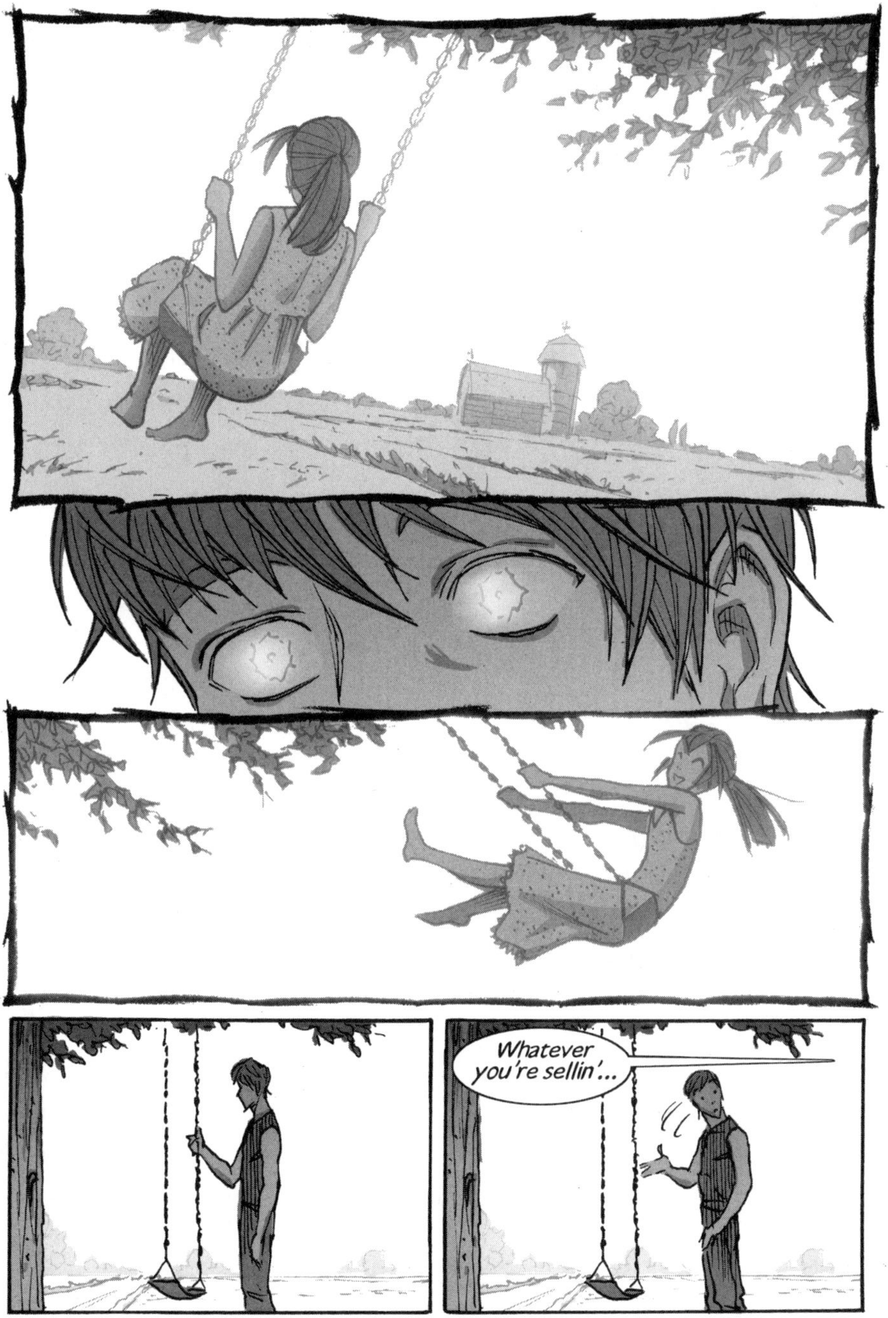
Whatever you're sellin'...

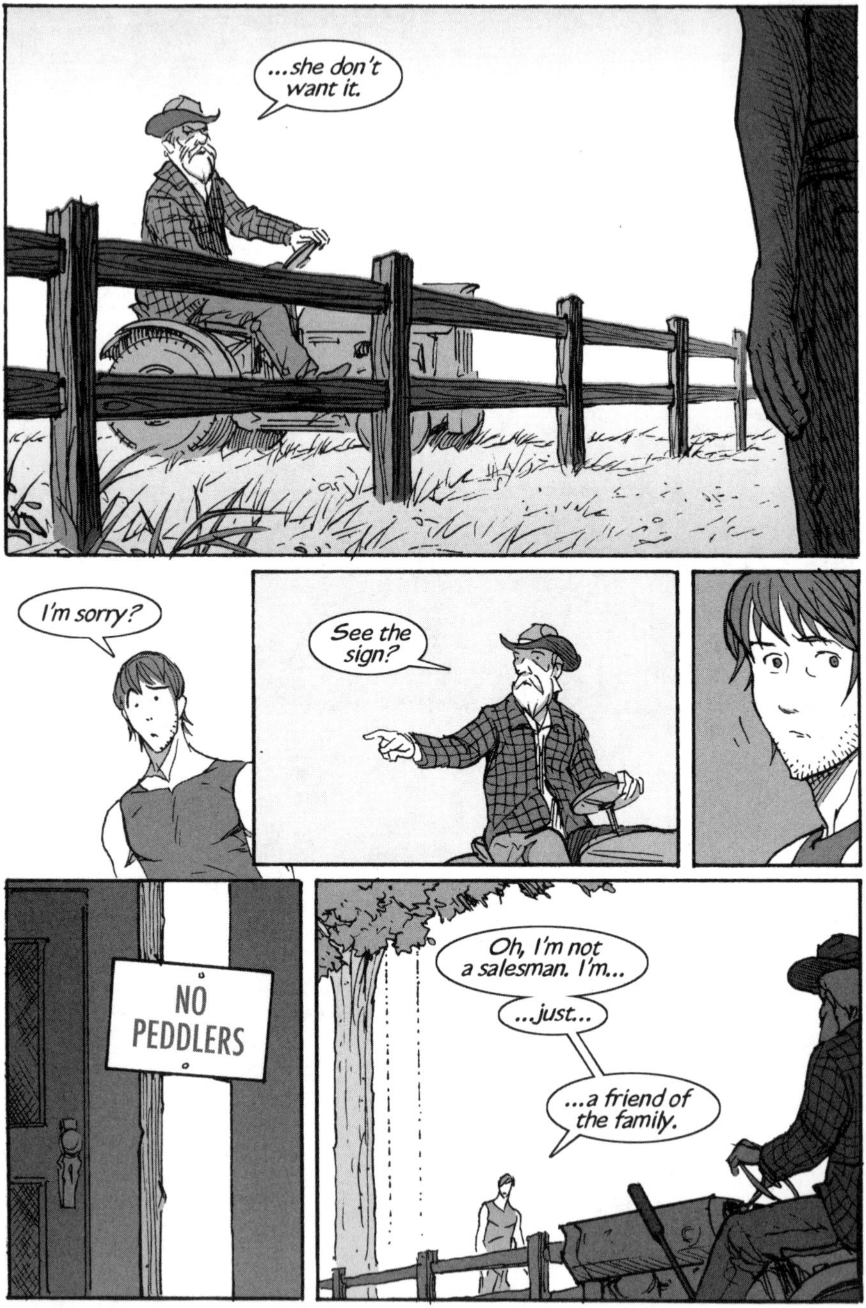
...she don't want it.
I'm sorry?
See the sign?
NO PEDDLERS
Oh, I'm not a salesman. I'm...
...just...
...a friend of the family.

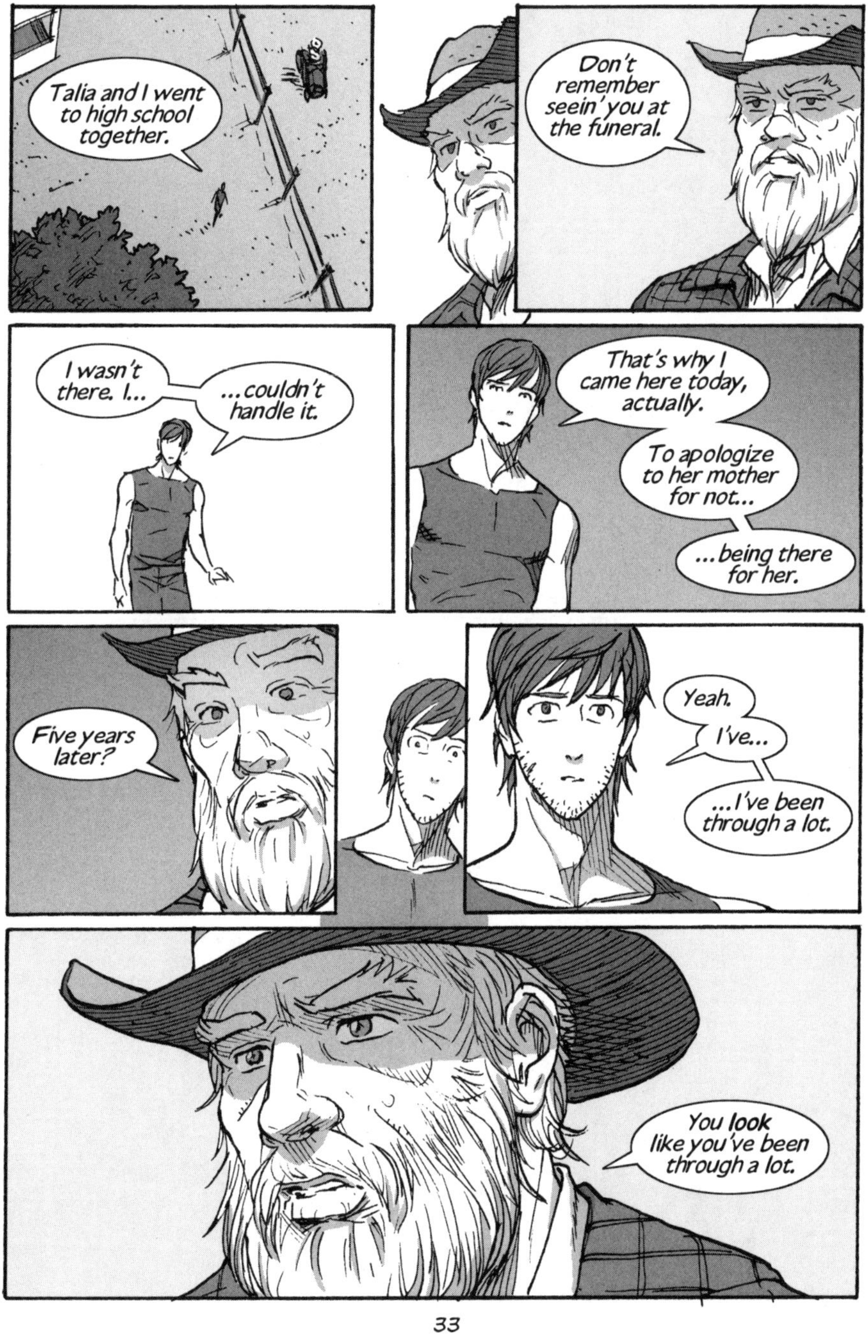
Talia and I went to high school together.
Don't remember seein' you at the funeral.
I wasn't there. I...
...couldn't handle it.
That's why I came here today, actually.
To apologize to her mother for not...
...being there for her.
Five years later?
Yeah.
I've...
...I've been through a lot.
You **look** like you've been through a lot.

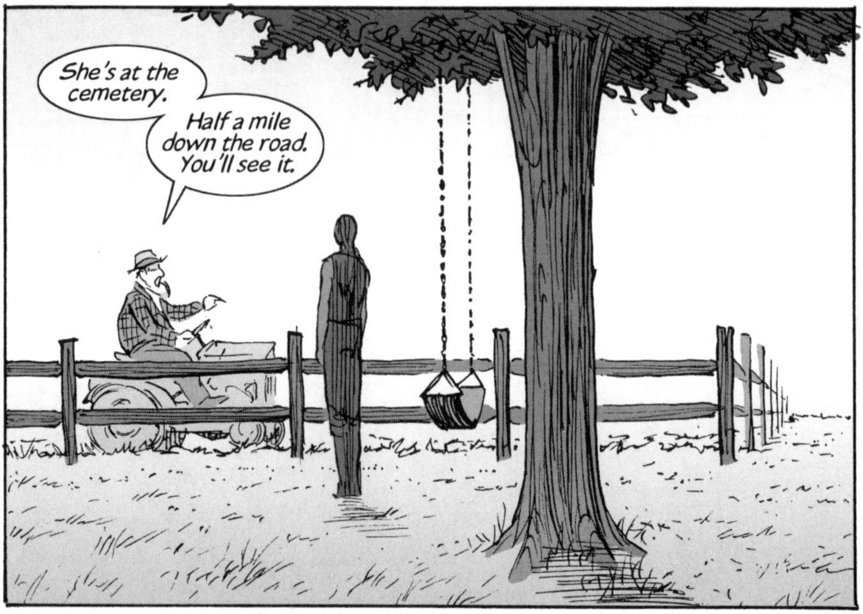
She's at the cemetery.
Half a mile down the road. You'll see it.

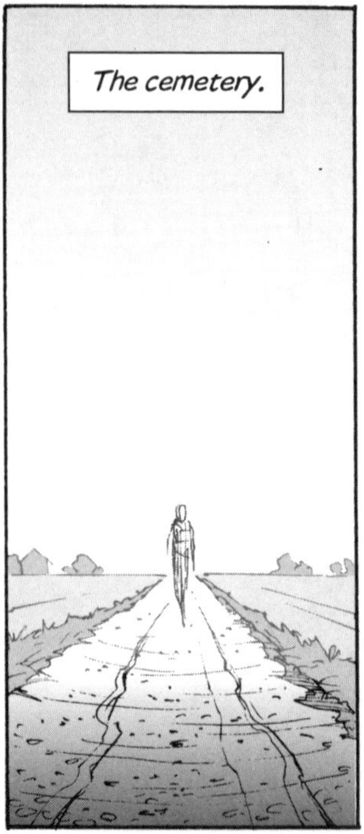
The cemetery.

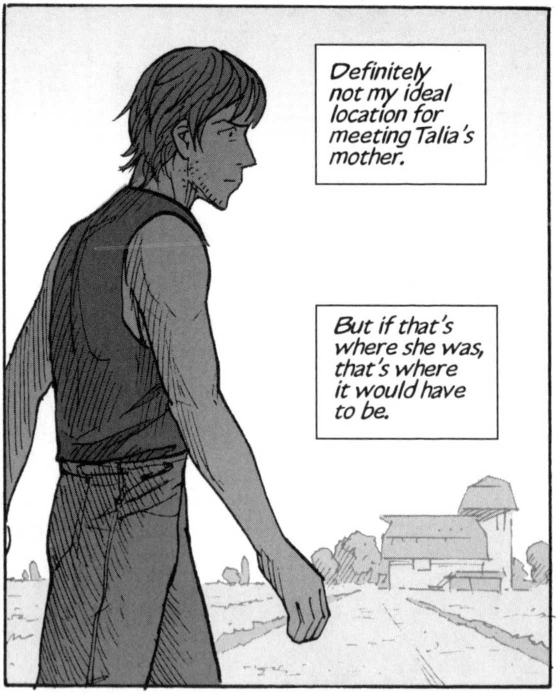
Definitely not my ideal location for meeting Talia's mother.
But if that's where she was, that's where it would have to be.

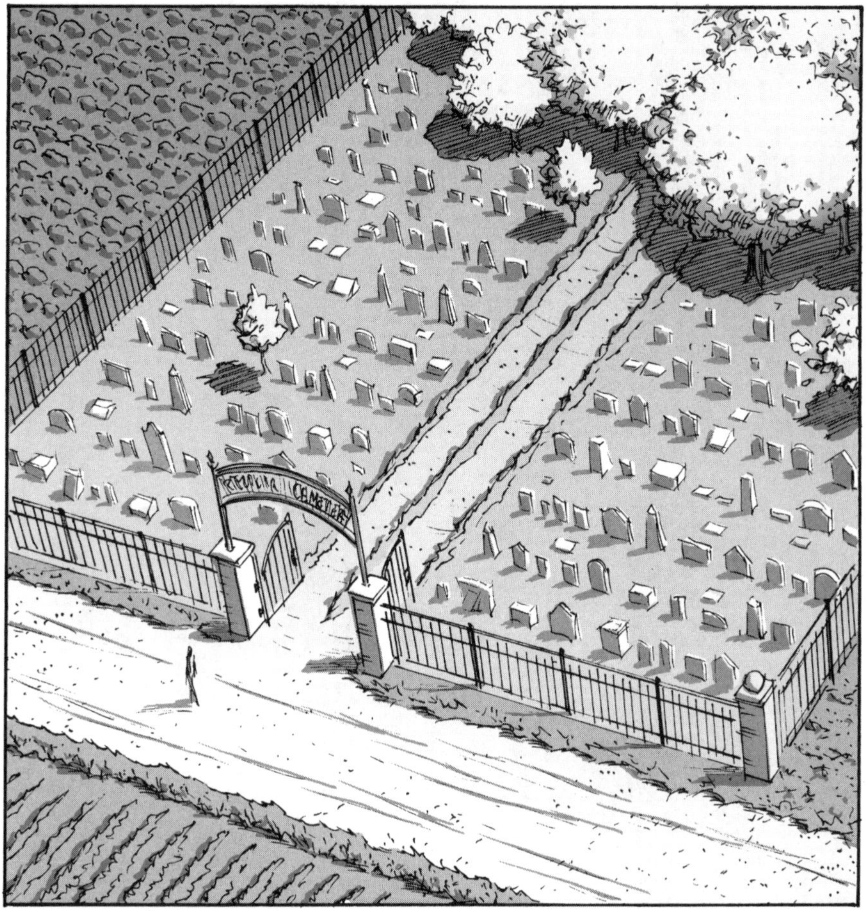
CEMETERY

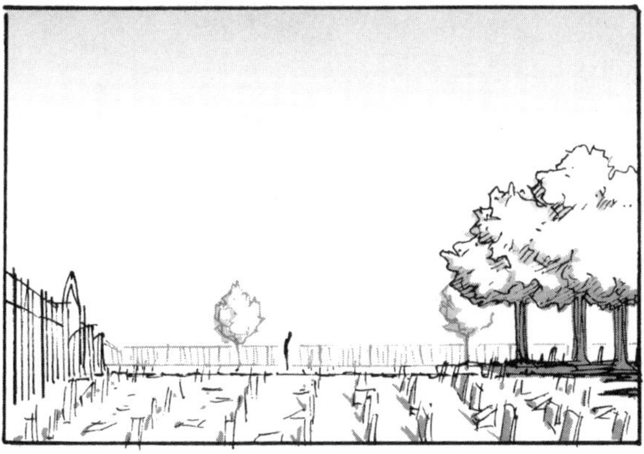

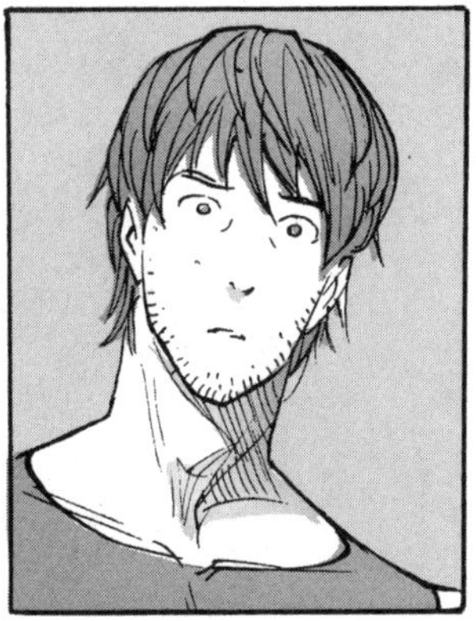

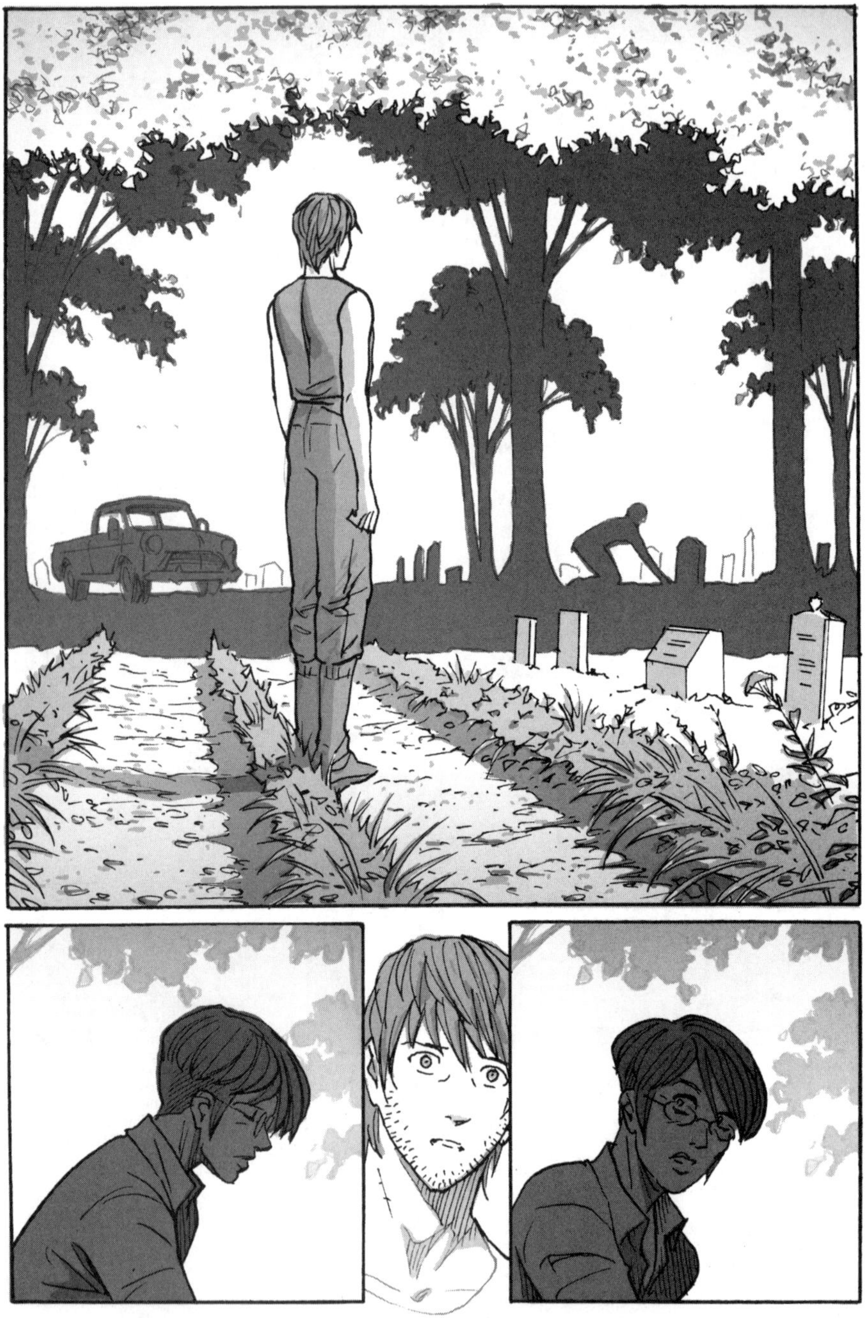

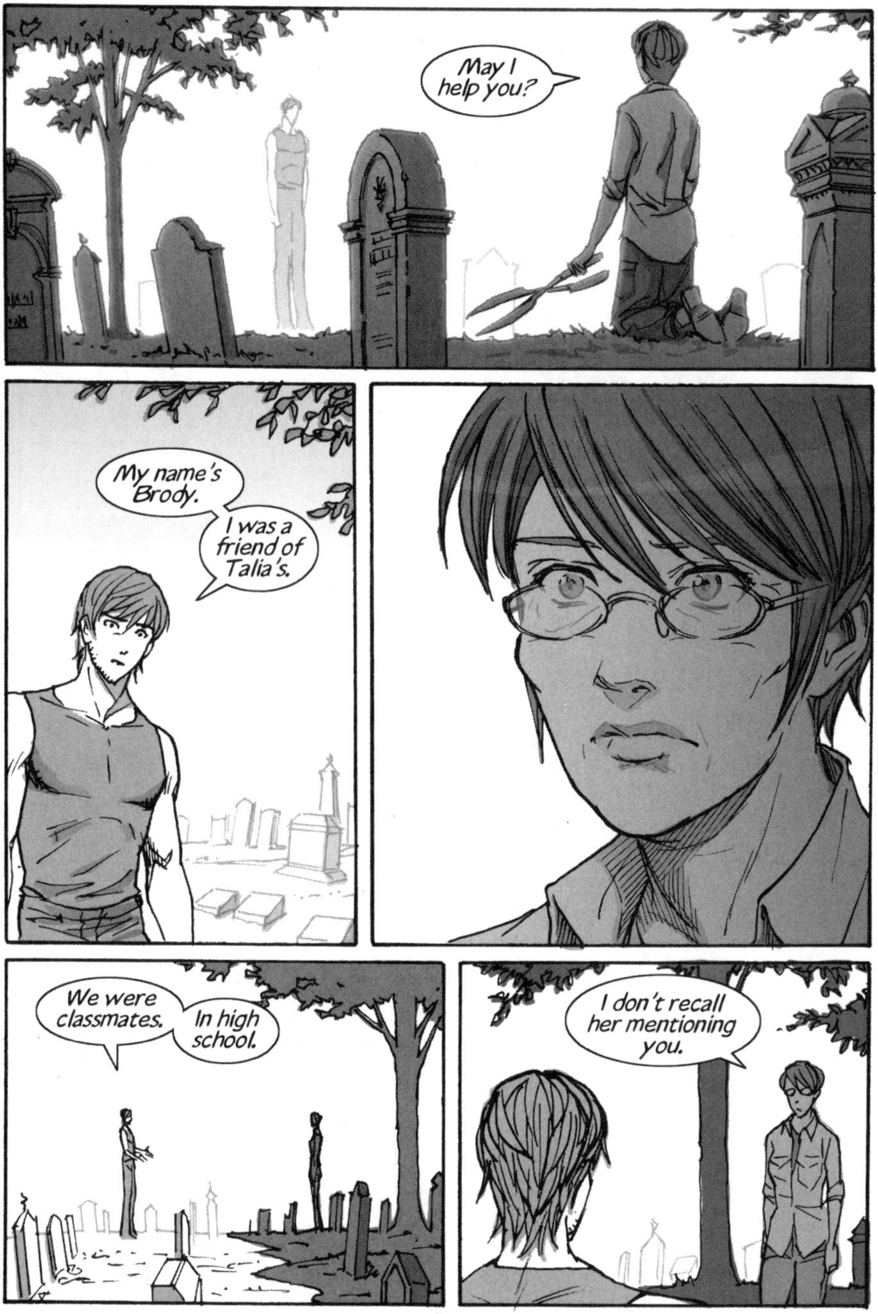
May I help you?
My name's Brody.
I was a friend of Talia's.
We were classmates.
In high school.
I don't recall her mentioning you.

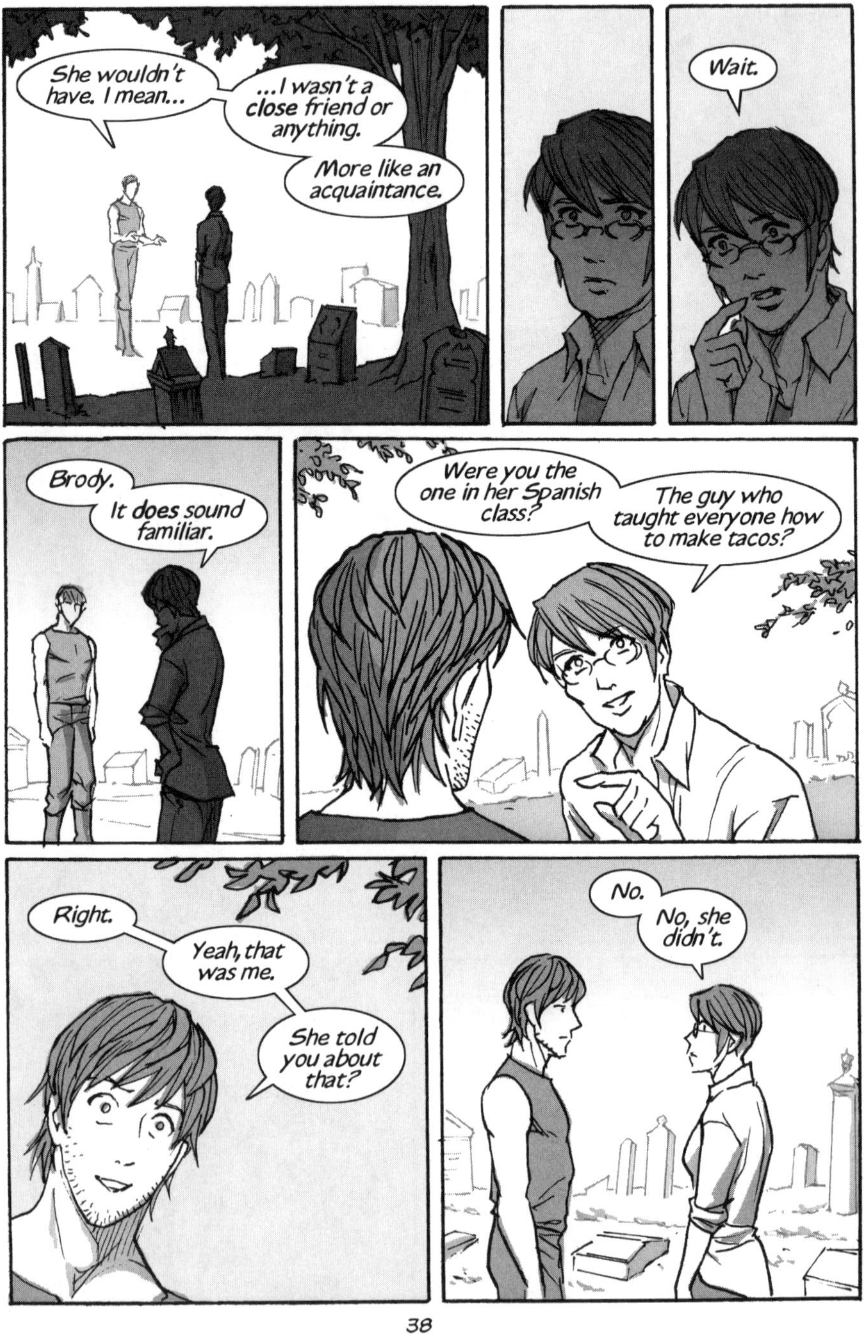
She wouldn't have. I mean...
...I wasn't a close friend or anything.
More like an acquaintance.
Wait.
Brody.
It does sound familiar.
Were you the one in her Spanish class?
The guy who taught everyone how to make tacos?
Right.
Yeah, that was me.
She told you about that?
No.
No, she didn't.

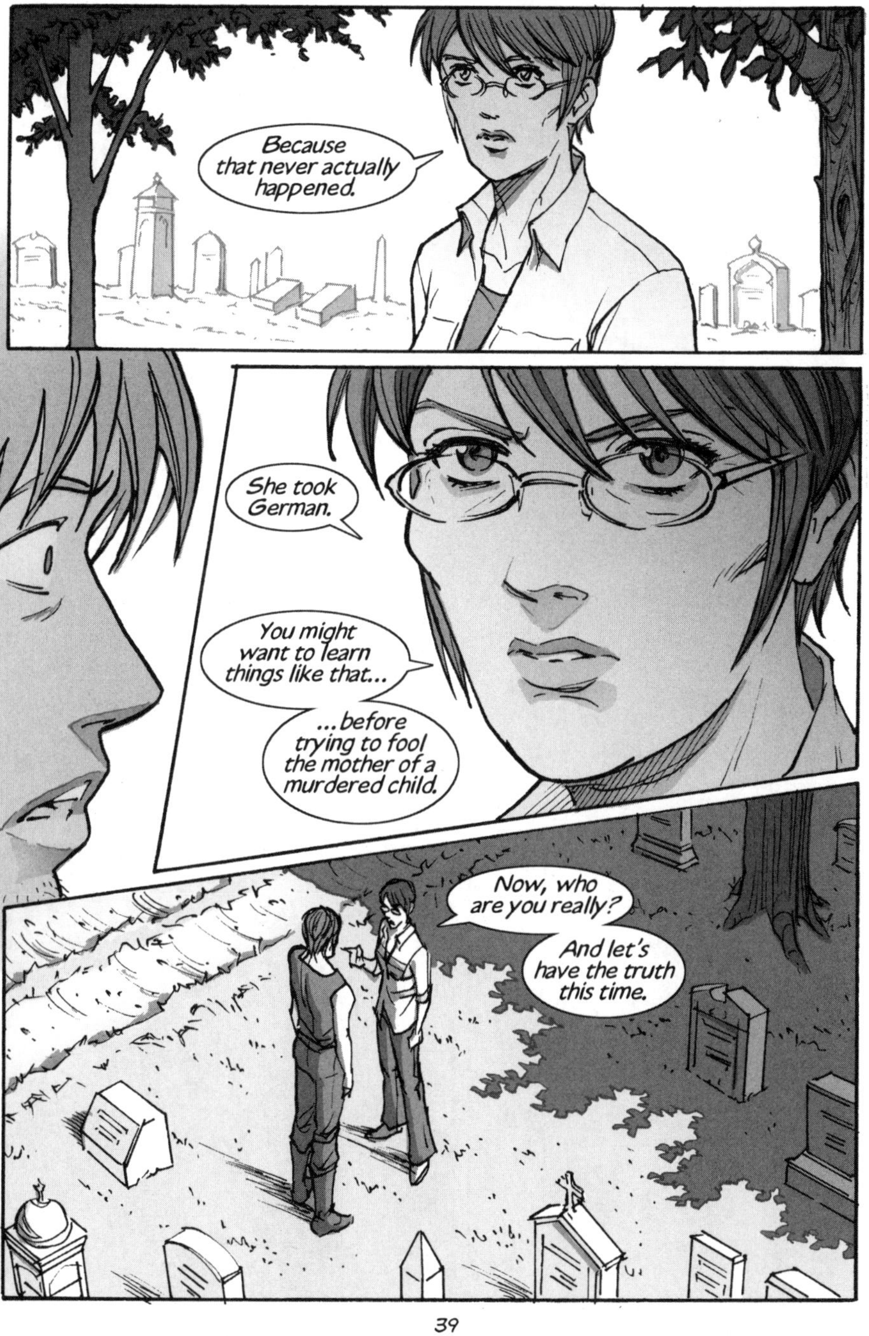
Because that never actually happened.
She took German.
You might want to learn things like that...
...before trying to fool the mother of a murdered child.
Now, who are you really?
And let's have the truth this time.

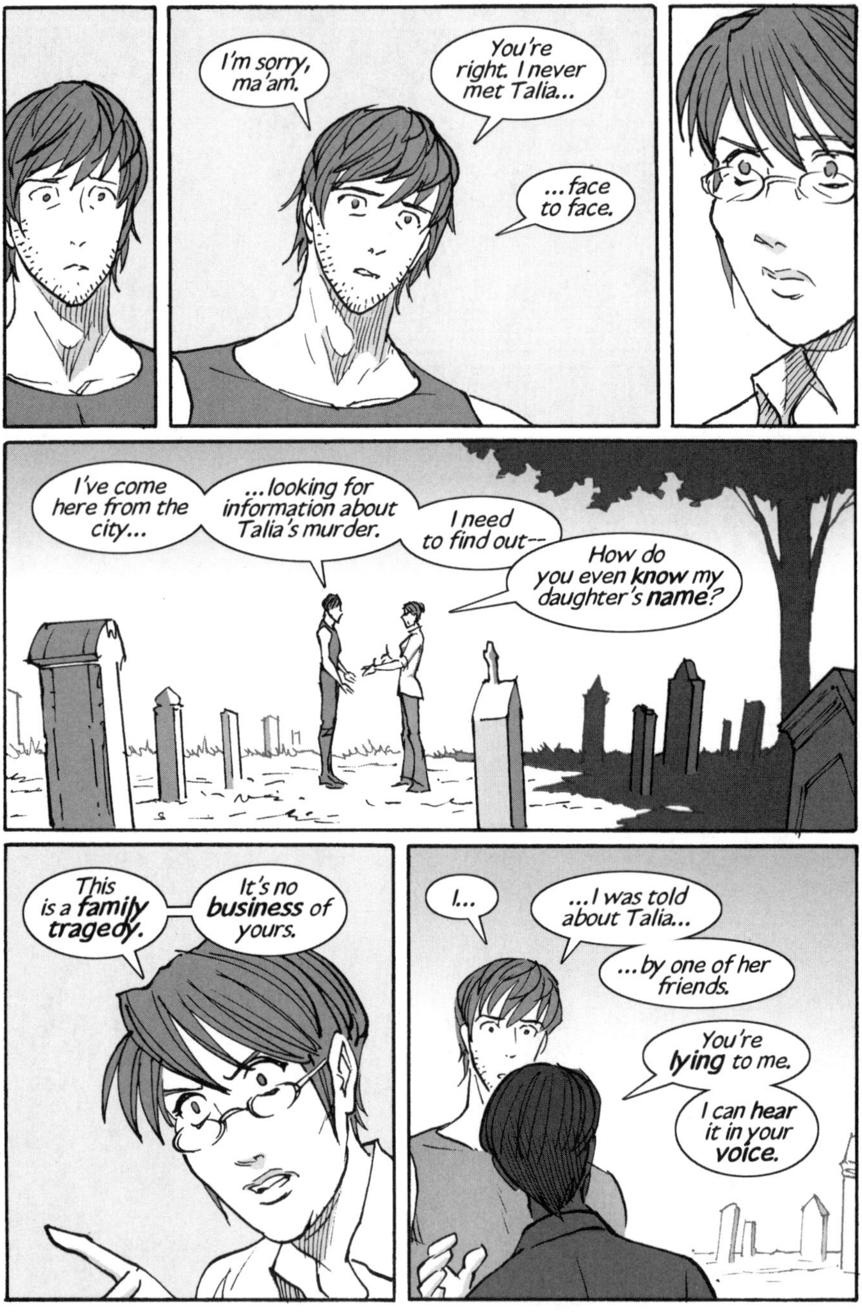
I'm sorry, ma'am.
You're right. I never met Talia...
...face to face.
I've come here from the city...
...looking for information about Talia's murder.
I need to find out--
How do you even **know** my daughter's **name**?
This is a **family tragedy**.
It's no **business** of yours.
I...
...I was told about Talia...
...by one of her friends.
You're **lying** to me.
I can **hear** it in your **voice**.

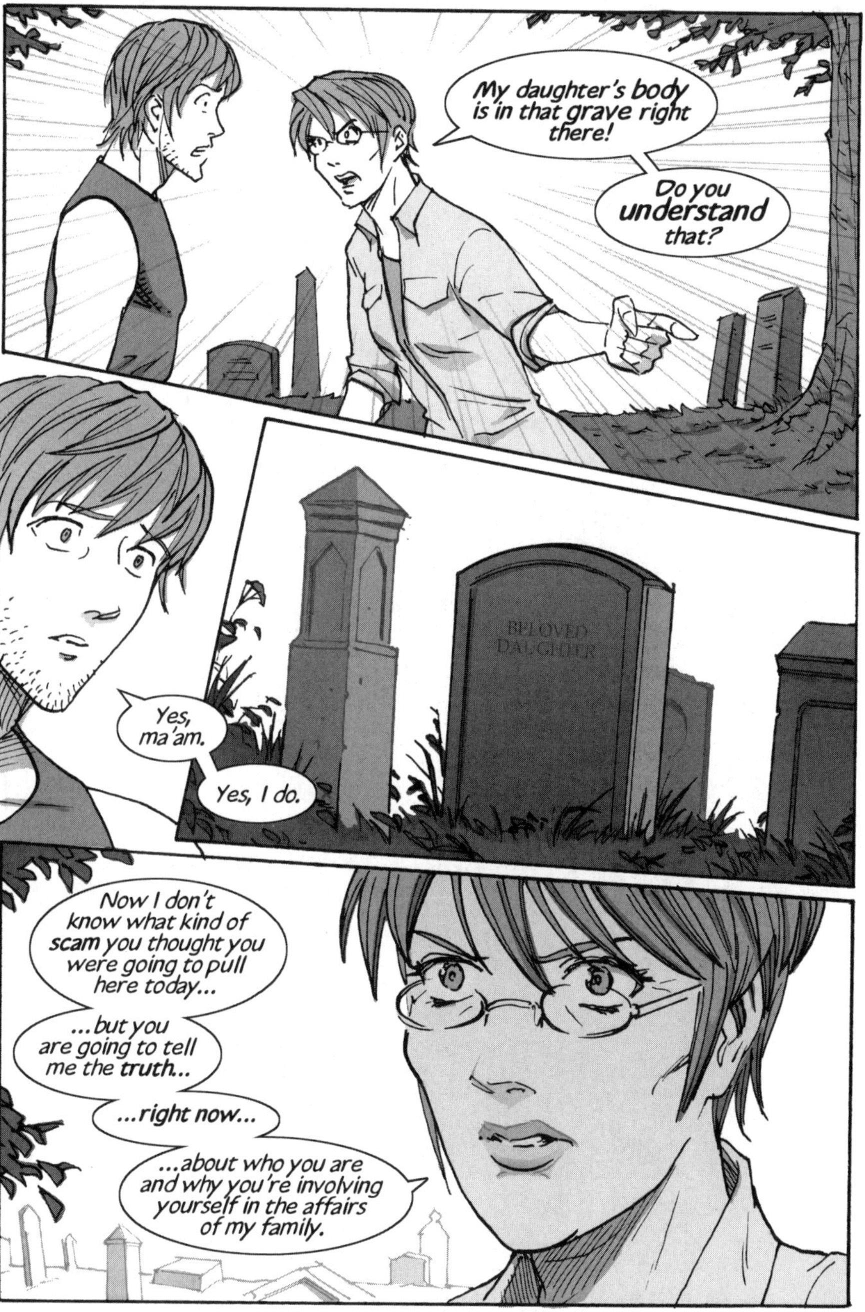
My daughter's body is in that grave right there!
Do you **understand** that?
BELOVED DAUGHTER
Yes, ma'am.
Yes, I do.
Now I don't know what kind of **scam** you thought you were going to pull here today...
...but you are going to tell me the **truth**...
...**right now**...
...about who you are and why you're involving yourself in the affairs of my family.

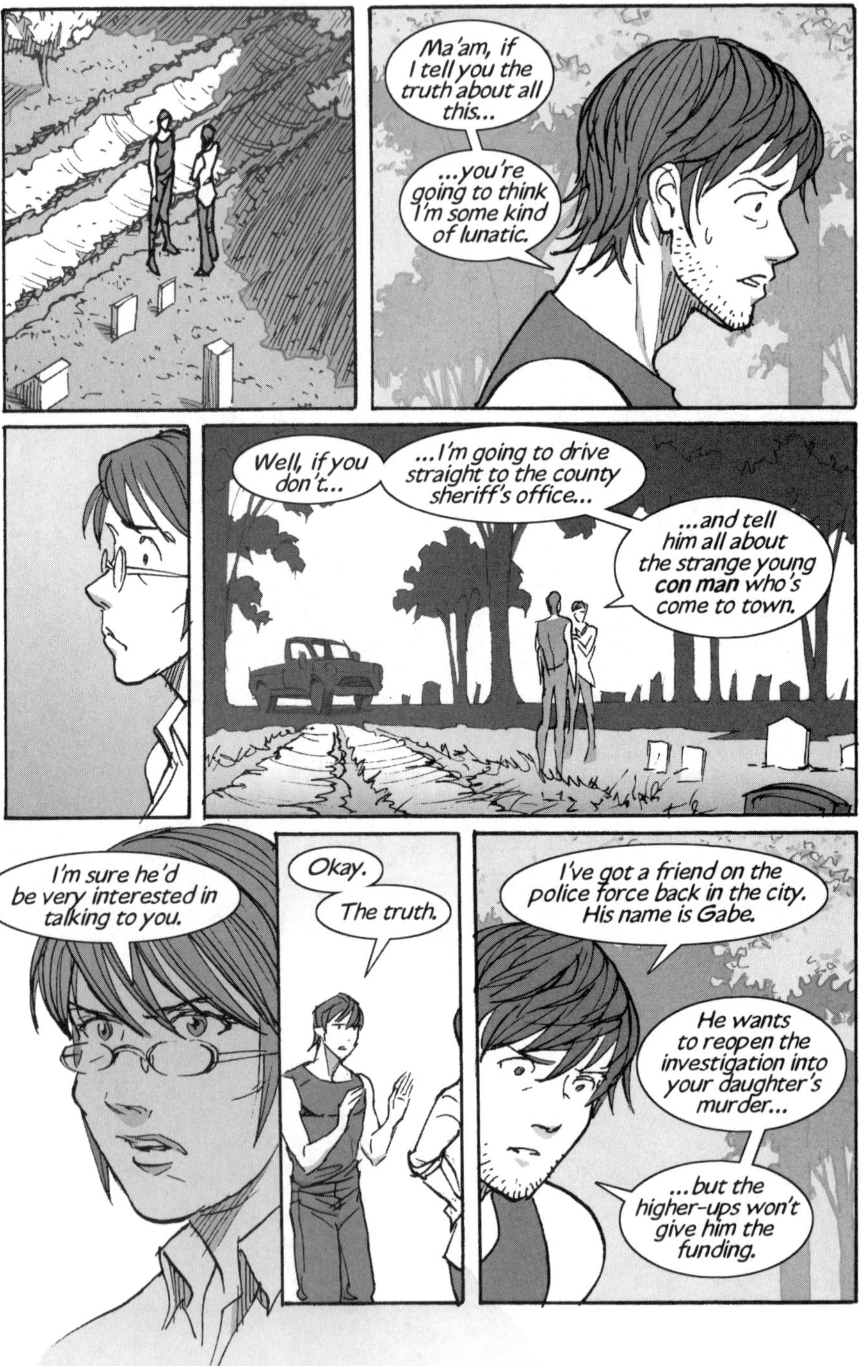
Ma'am, if I tell you the truth about all this...
...you're going to think I'm some kind of lunatic.
Well, if you don't...
...I'm going to drive straight to the county sheriff's office...
...and tell him all about the strange young **con man** who's come to town.
I'm sure he'd be very interested in talking to you.
Okay.
The truth.
I've got a friend on the police force back in the city. His name is Gabe.
He wants to reopen the investigation into your daughter's murder...
...but the higher-ups won't give him the funding.

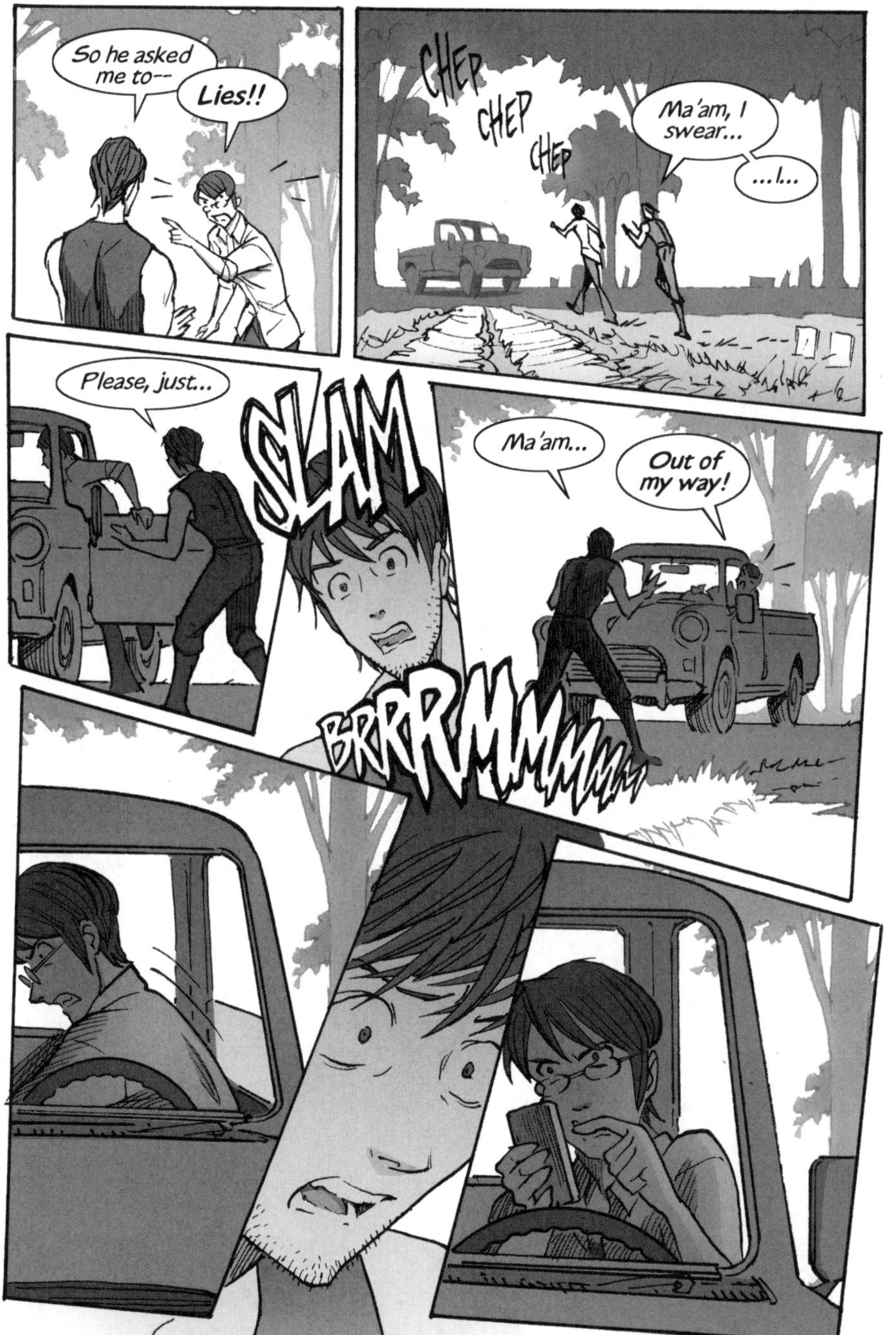
So he asked me to--
Lies!!
CHEP
CHEP
CHEP
Ma'am, I swear...
...I...
Please, just...
SLAM
Ma'am...
Out of my way!
BRRRMMMMM

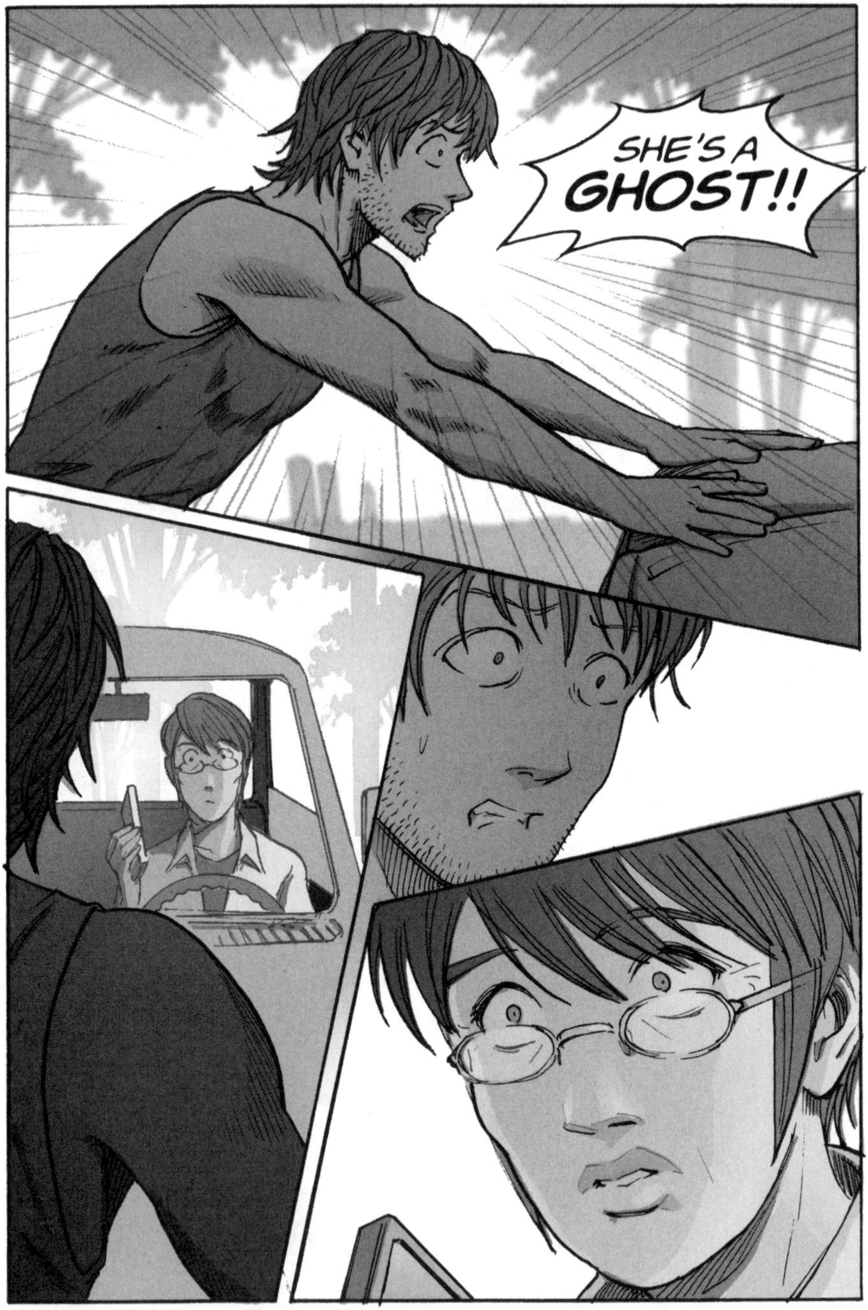
SHE'S A GHOST!!

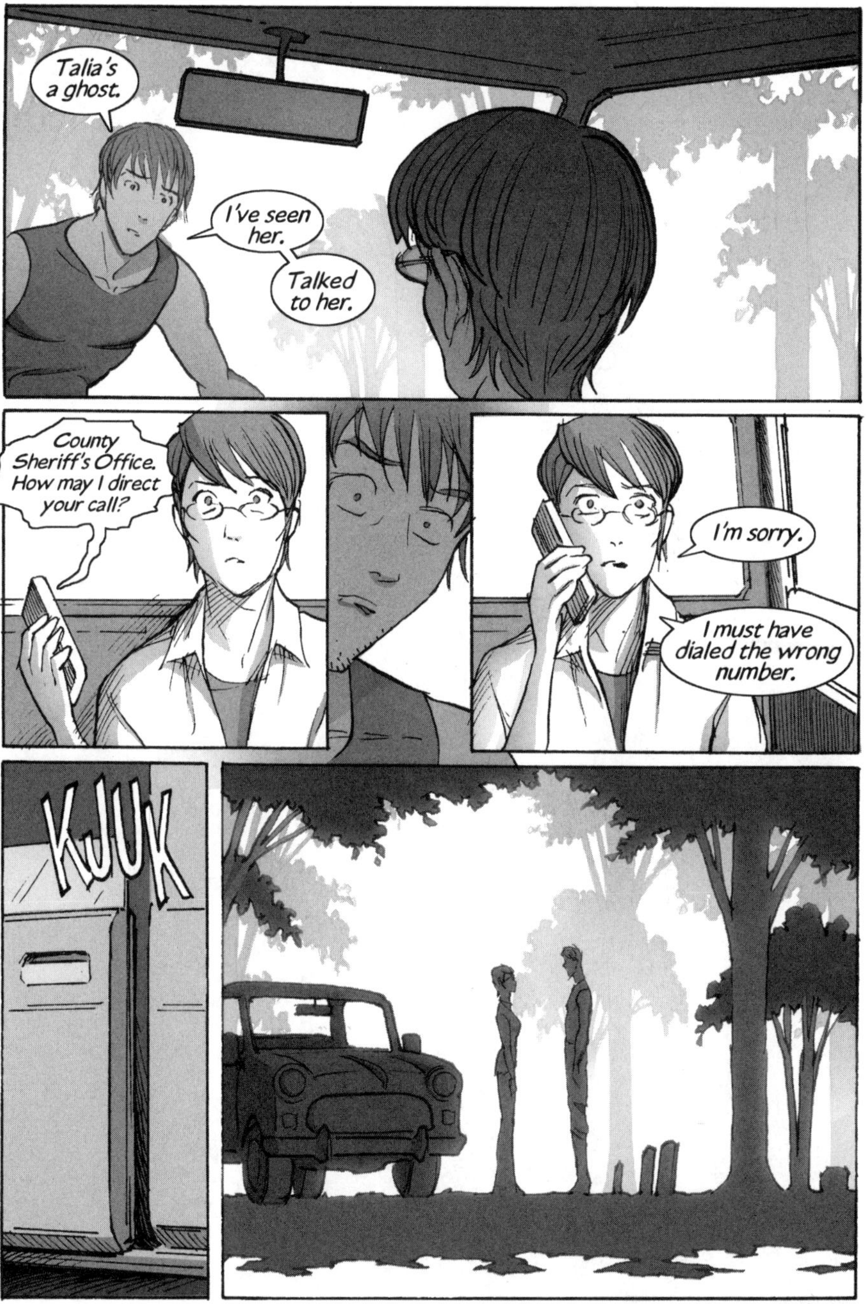
Talia's a ghost.
I've seen her.
Talked to her.
County Sheriff's Office. How may I direct your call?
I'm sorry.
I must have dialed the wrong number.
KJUK

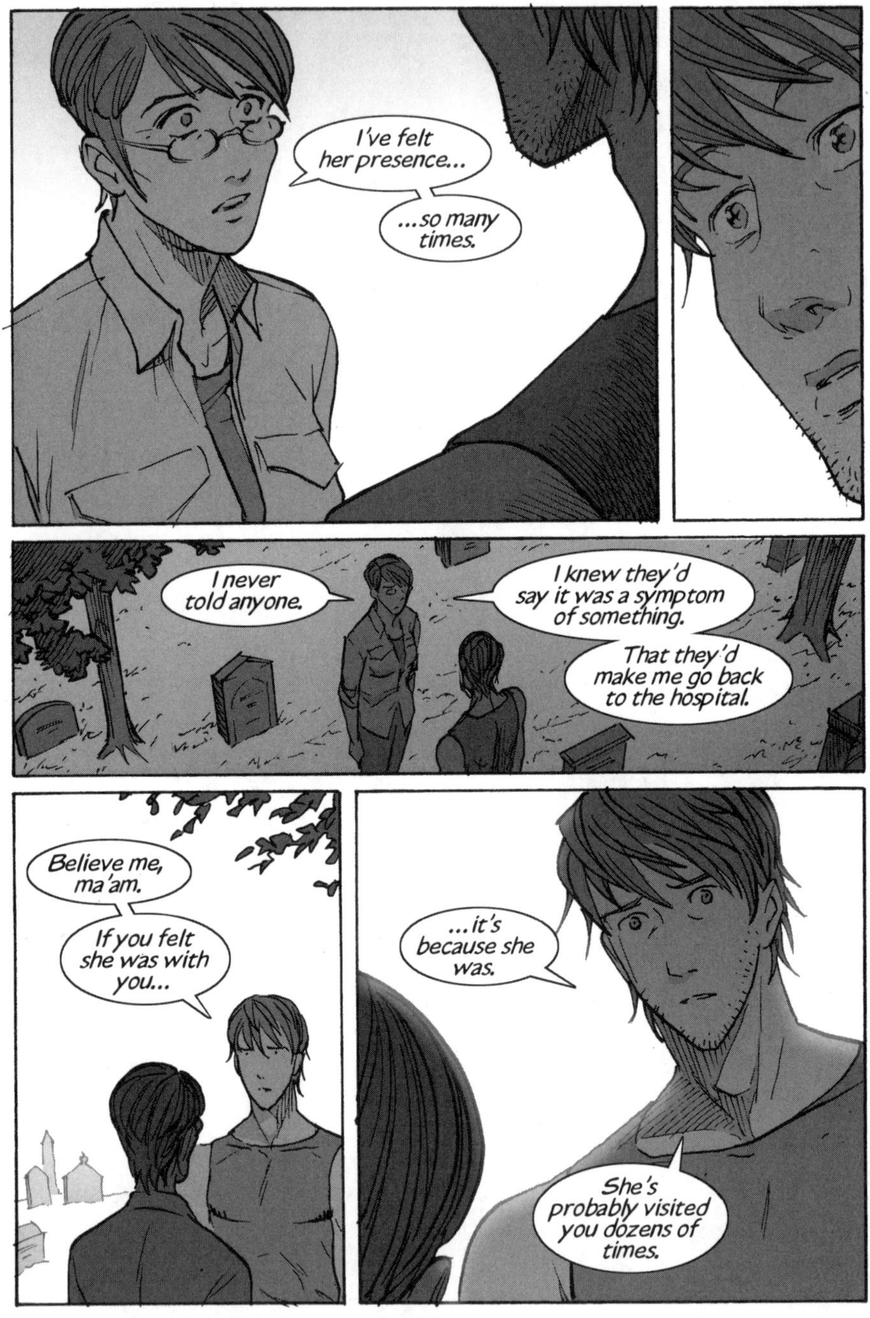
I've felt her presence...
...so many times.
I never told anyone.
I knew they'd say it was a symptom of something.
That they'd make me go back to the hospital.
Believe me, ma'am.
If you felt she was with you...
...it's because she was.
She's probably visited you dozens of times.

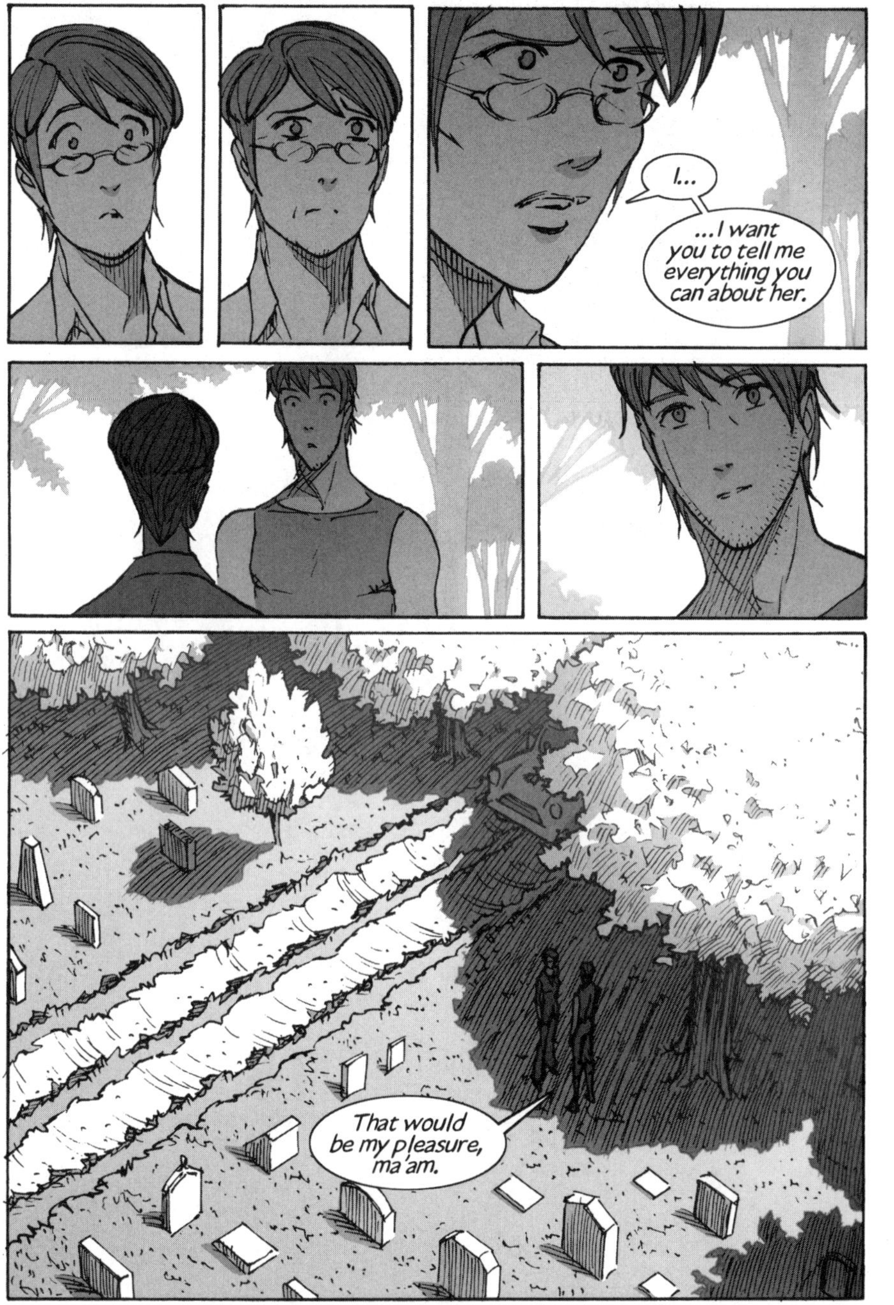
I...
...I want you to tell me everything you can about her.
That would be my pleasure, ma'am.

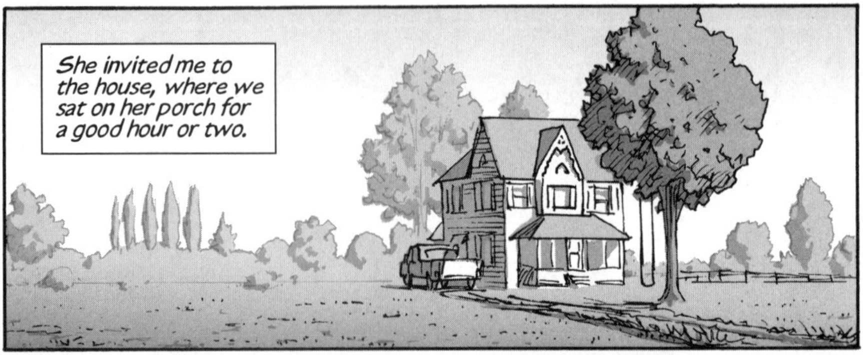
She invited me to the house, where we sat on her porch for a good hour or two.

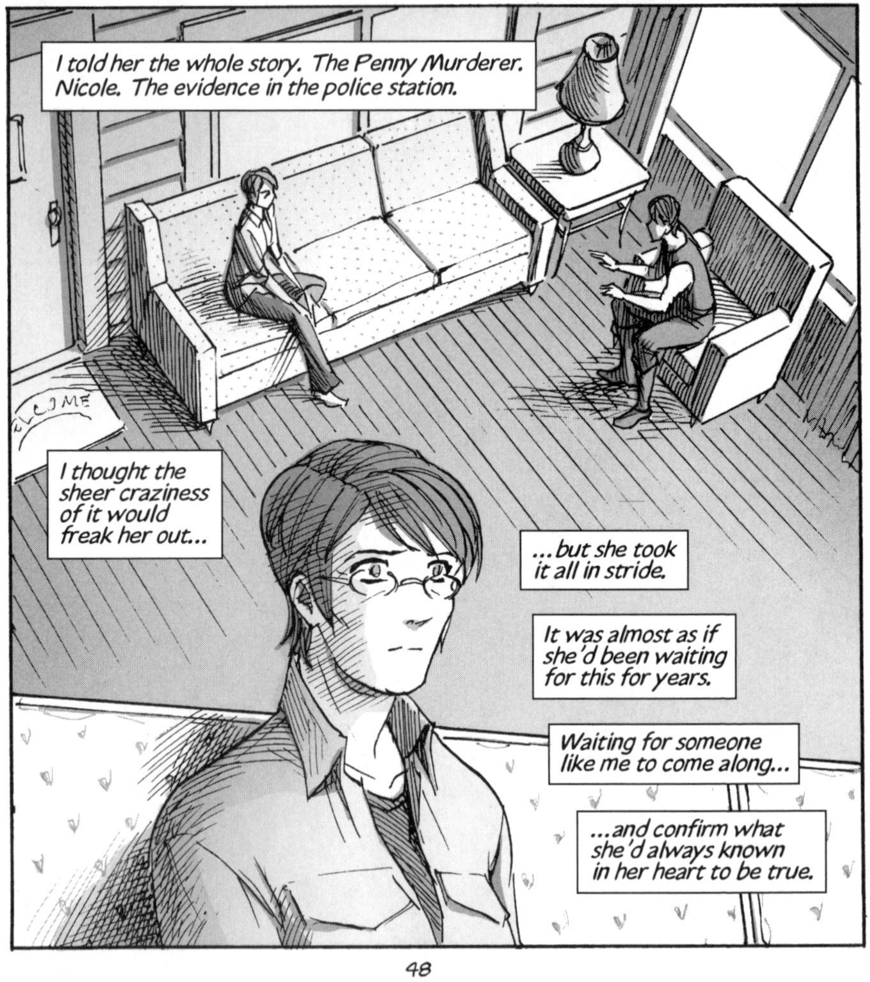
I told her the whole story. The Penny Murderer. Nicole. The evidence in the police station.
I thought the sheer craziness of it would freak her out...
...but she took it all in stride.
It was almost as if she'd been waiting for this for years.
Waiting for someone like me to come along...
...and confirm what she'd always known in her heart to be true.

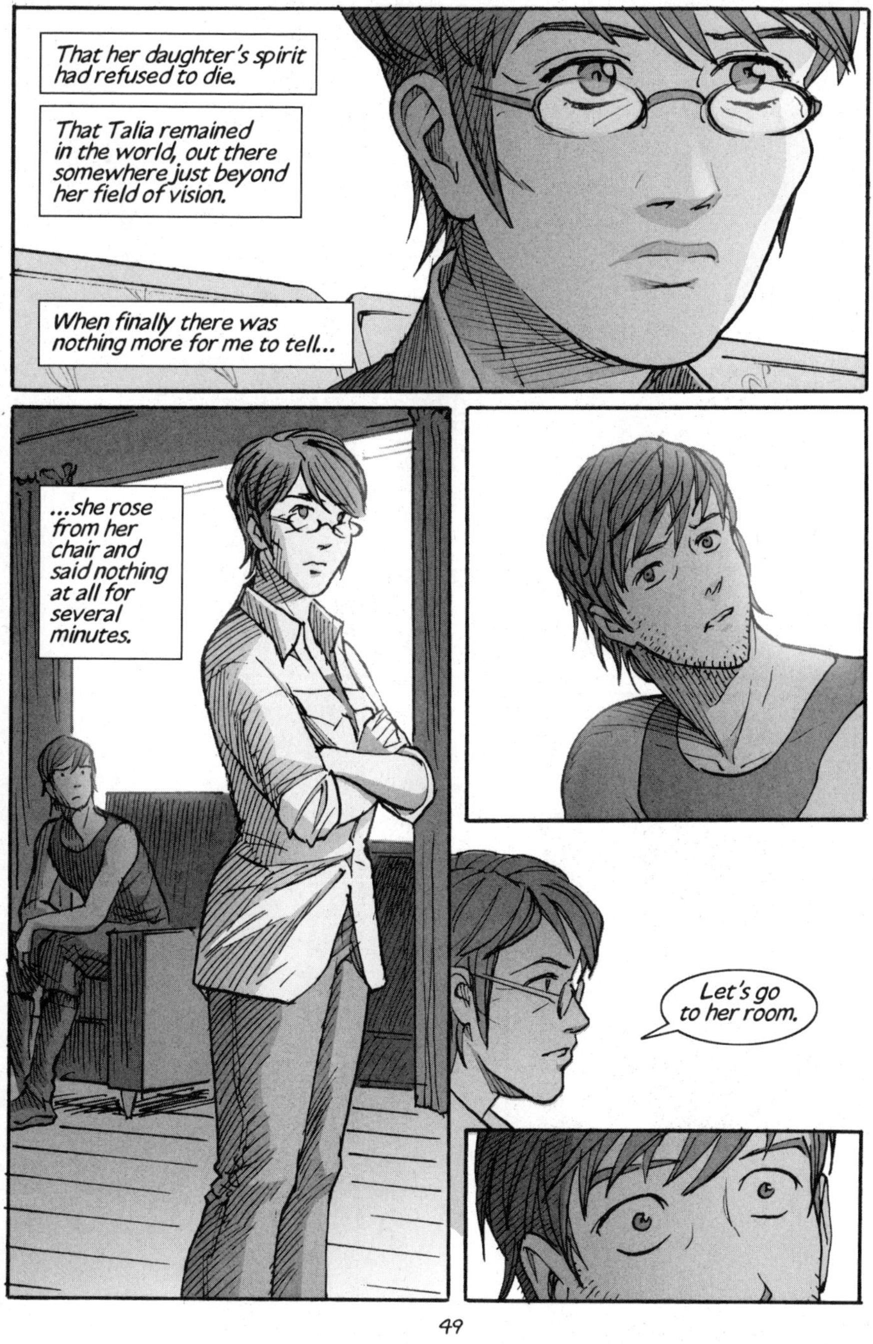
That her daughter's spirit had refused to die.
That Talia remained in the world, out there somewhere just beyond her field of vision.
When finally there was nothing more for me to tell...
...she rose from her chair and said nothing at all for several minutes.
Let's go to her room.

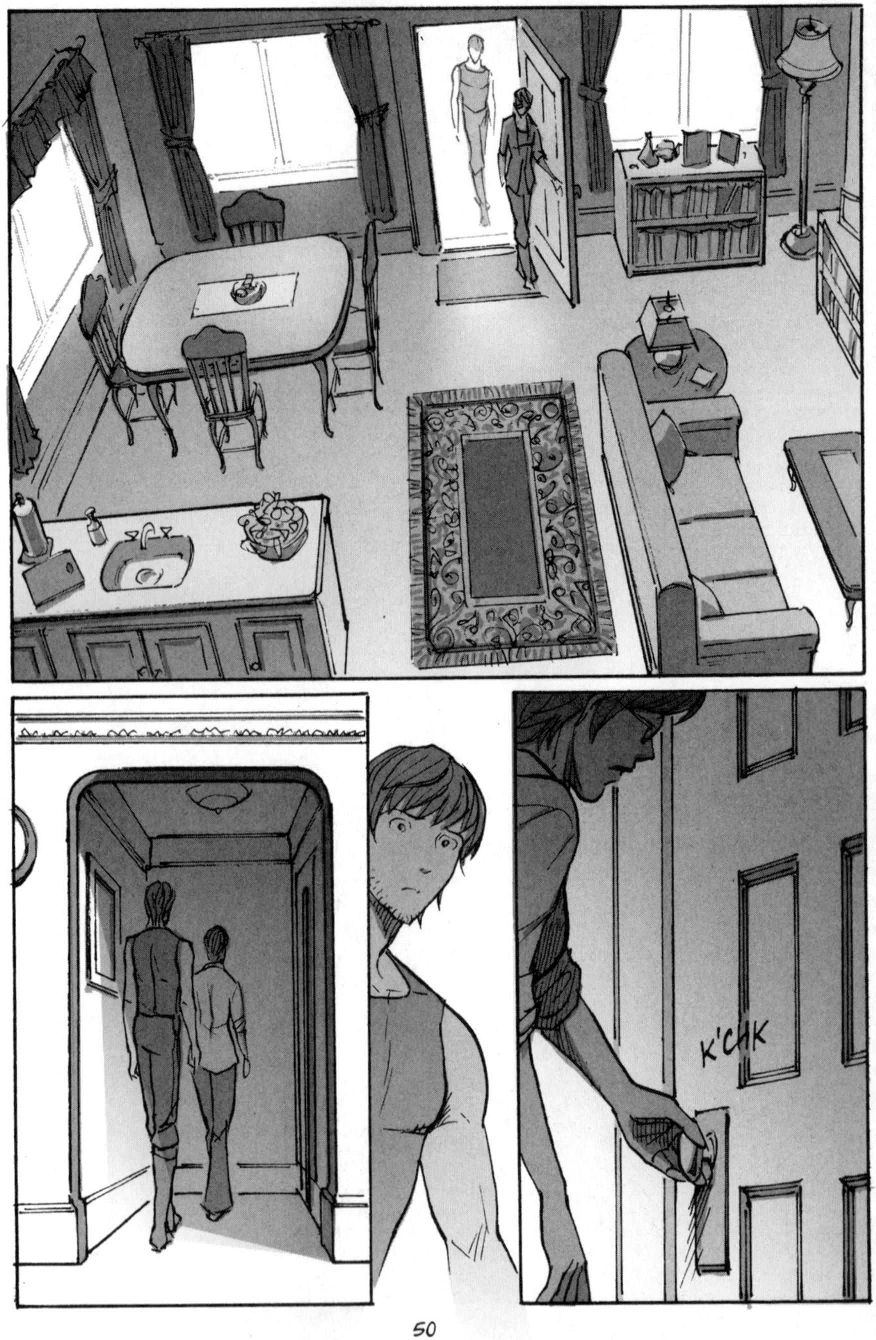
K'CHK

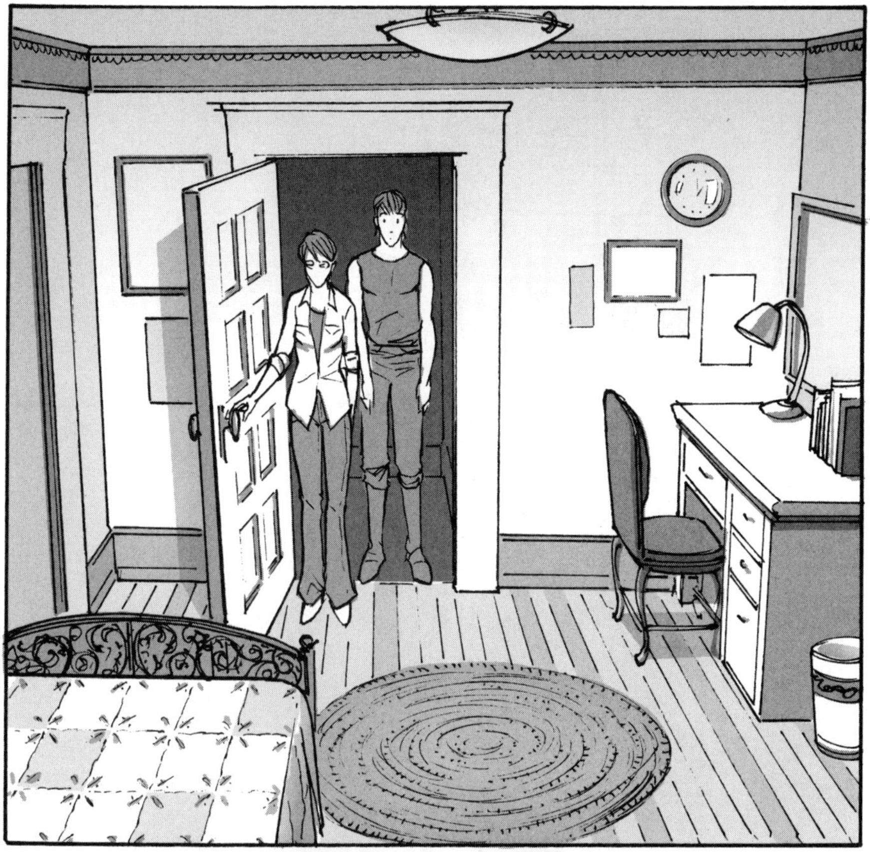

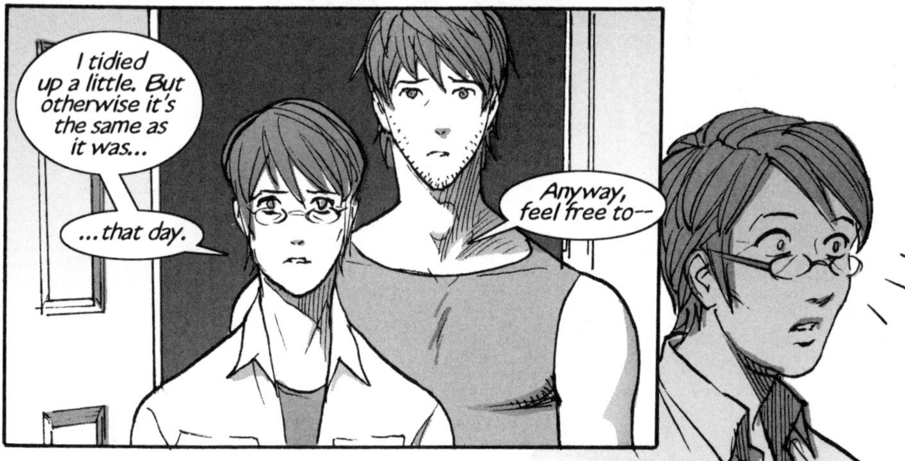
I tidied up a little. But otherwise it's the same as it was...
...that day.
Anyway, feel free to--

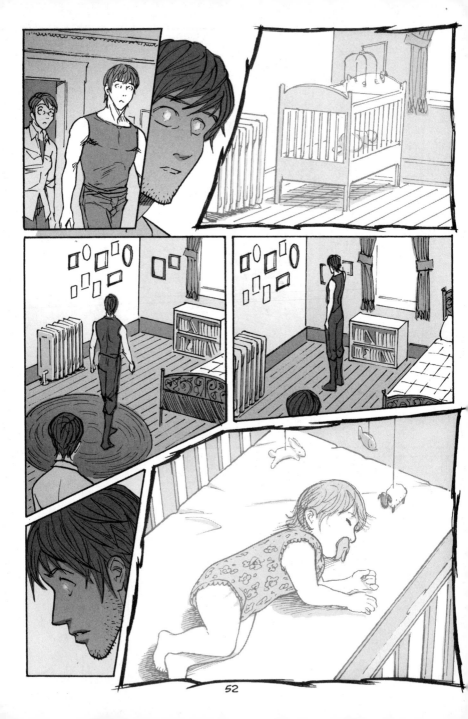

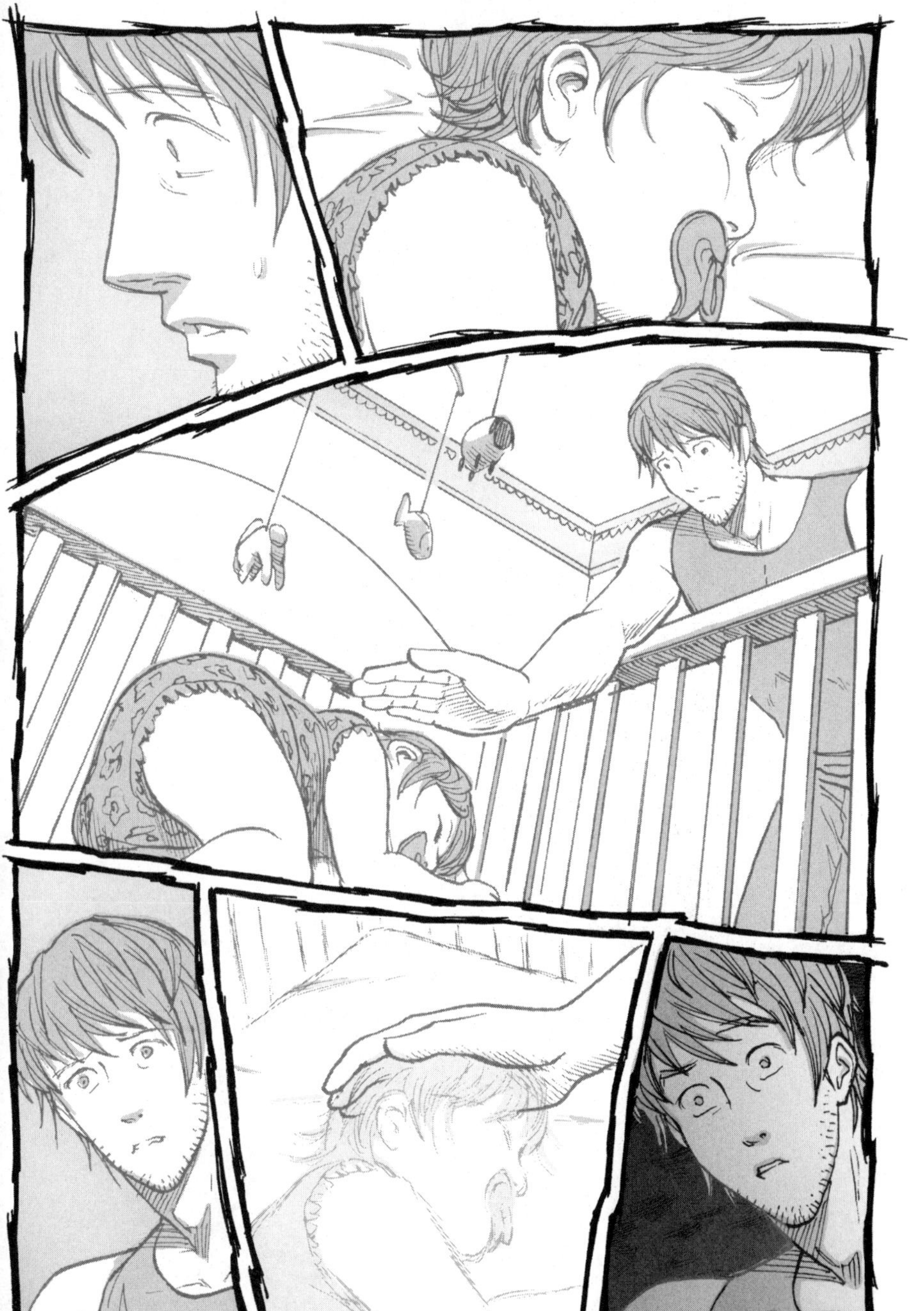

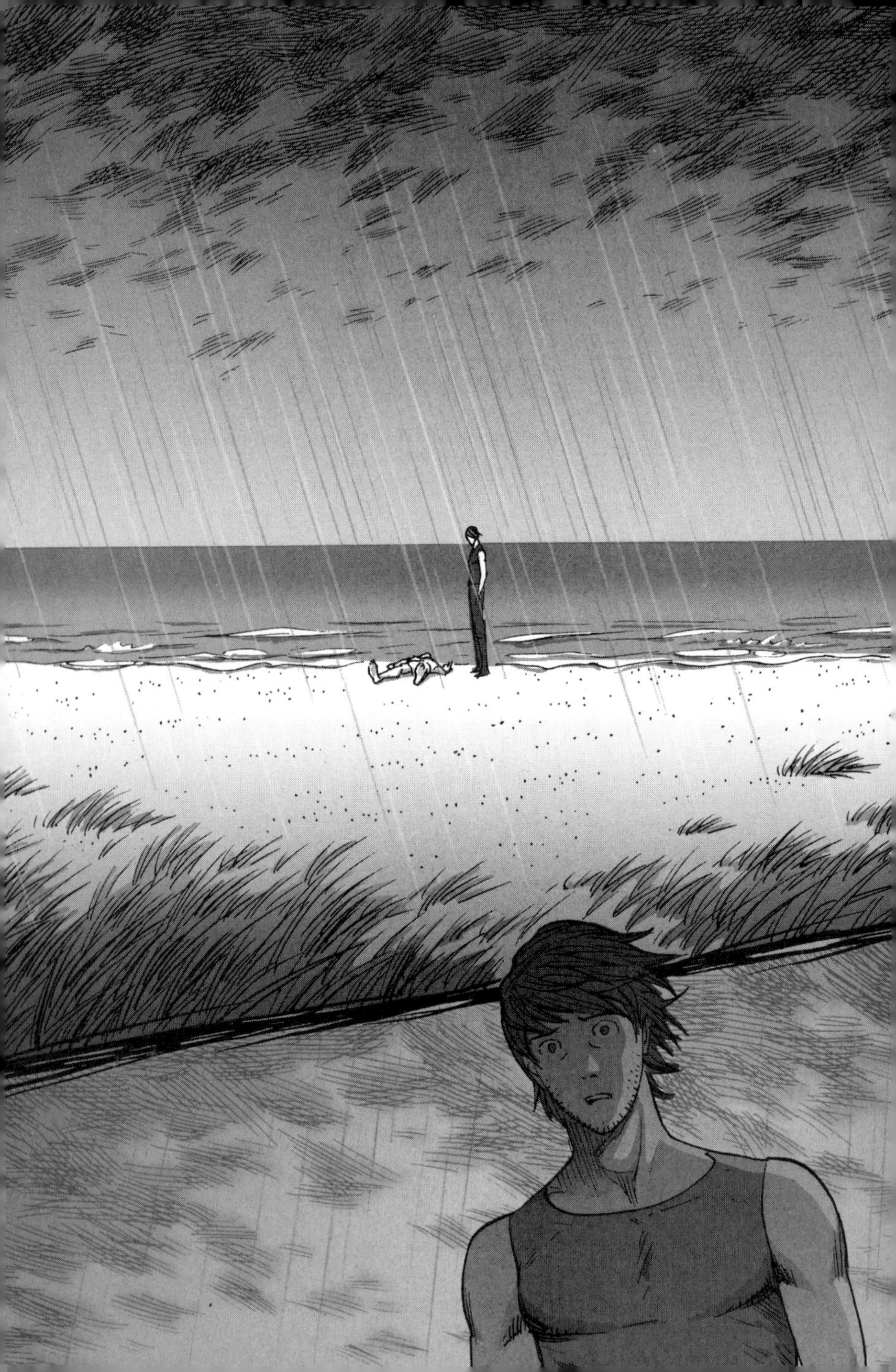

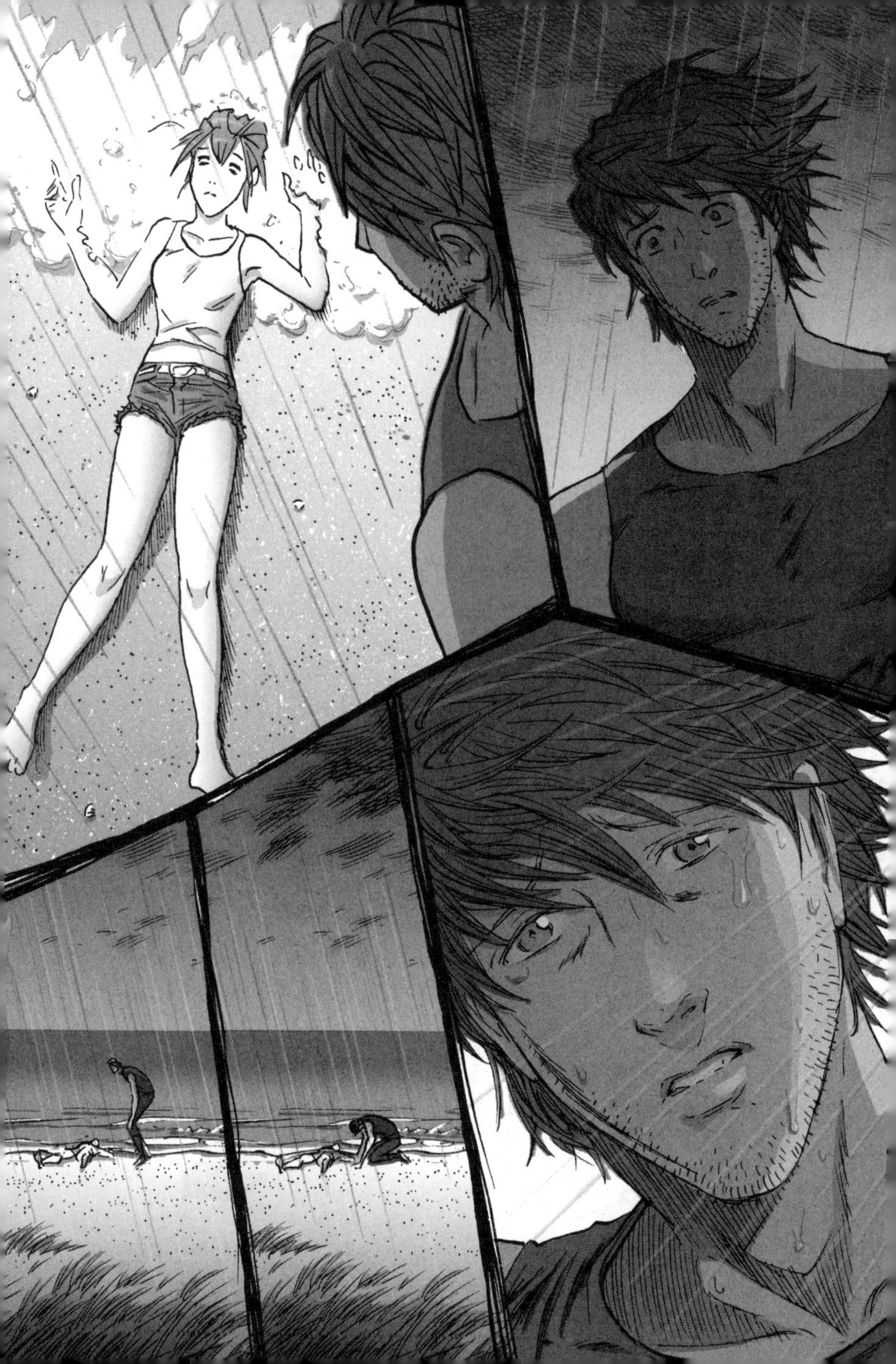

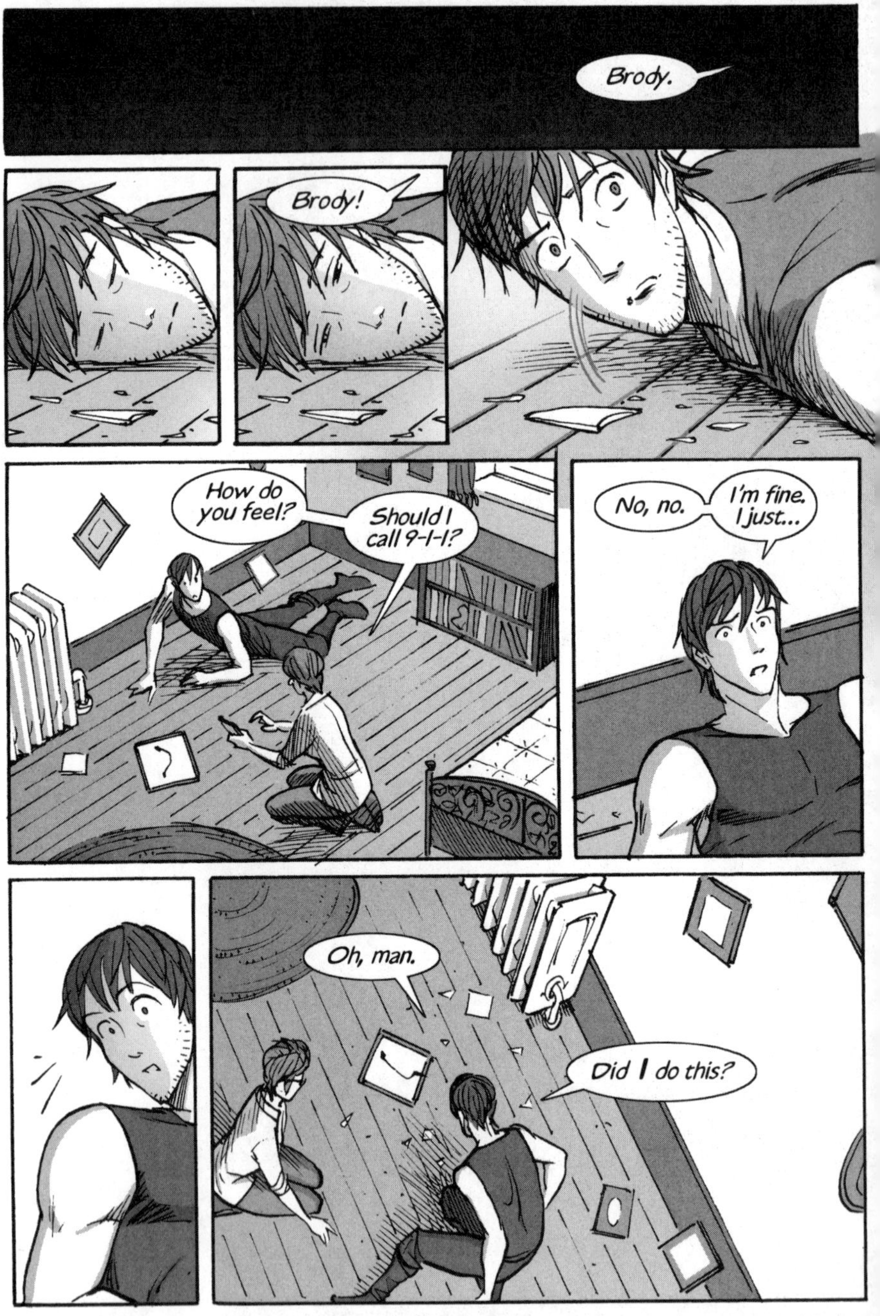
Brody.
Brody!
How do you feel?
Should I call 9-1-1?
No, no.
I'm fine. I just...
Oh, man.
Did I do this?

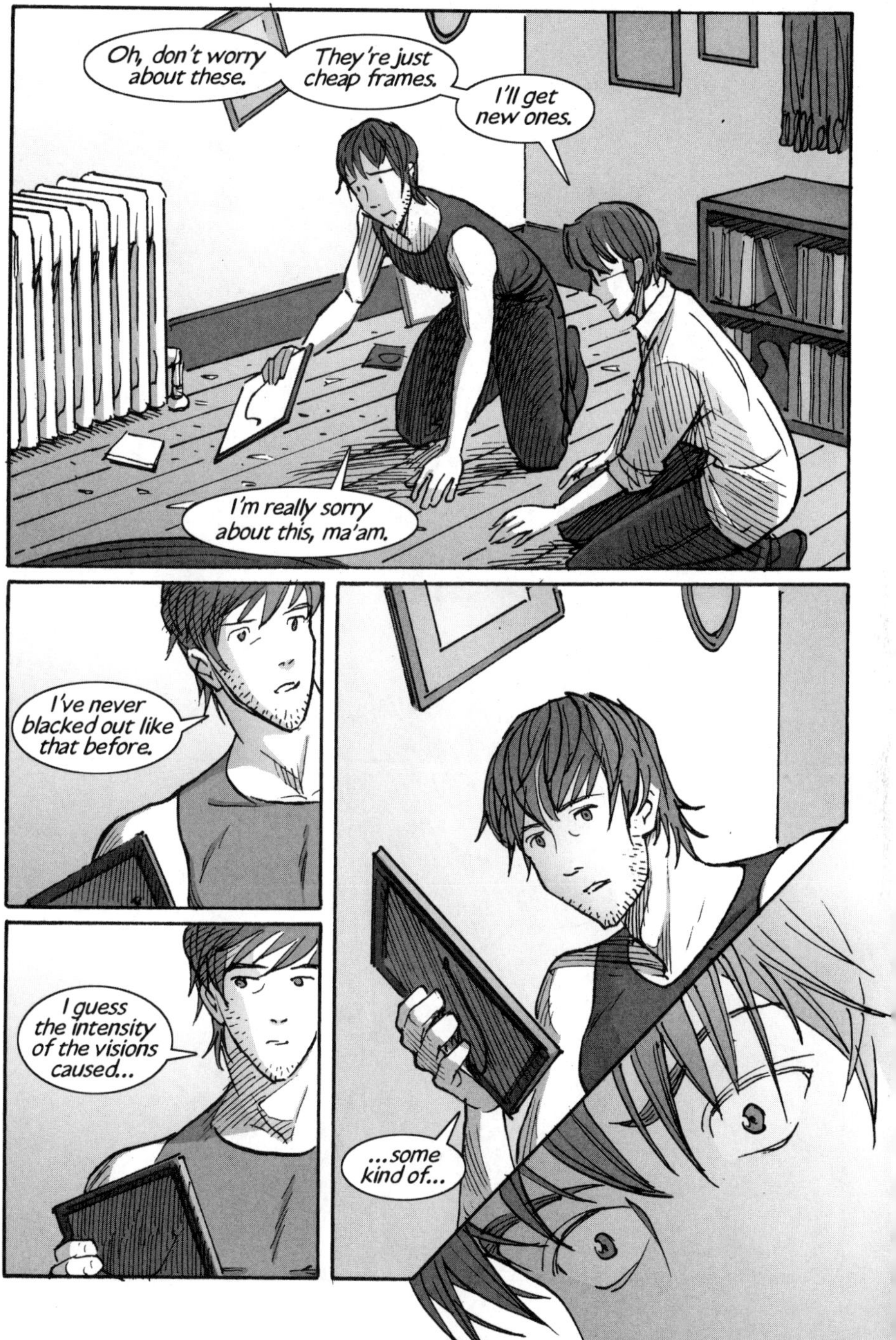
Oh, don't worry about these.
They're just cheap frames.
I'll get new ones.
I'm really sorry about this, ma'am.
I've never blacked out like that before.
I guess the intensity of the visions caused...
...some kind of...

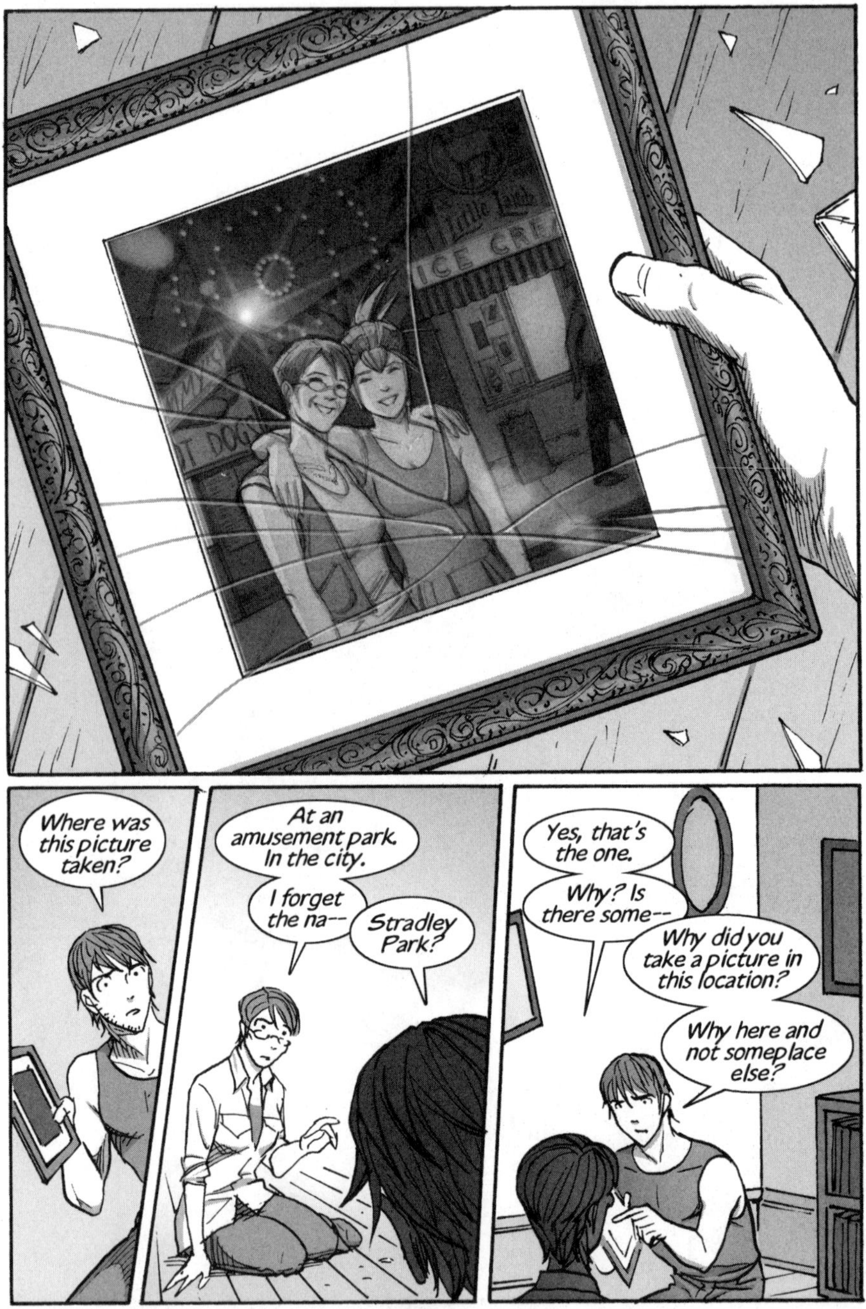
ICE CREA
Where was this picture taken?
At an amusement park. In the city.
I forget the na--
Stradley Park?
Yes, that's the one.
Why? Is there some--
Why did you take a picture in this location?
Why here and not someplace else?

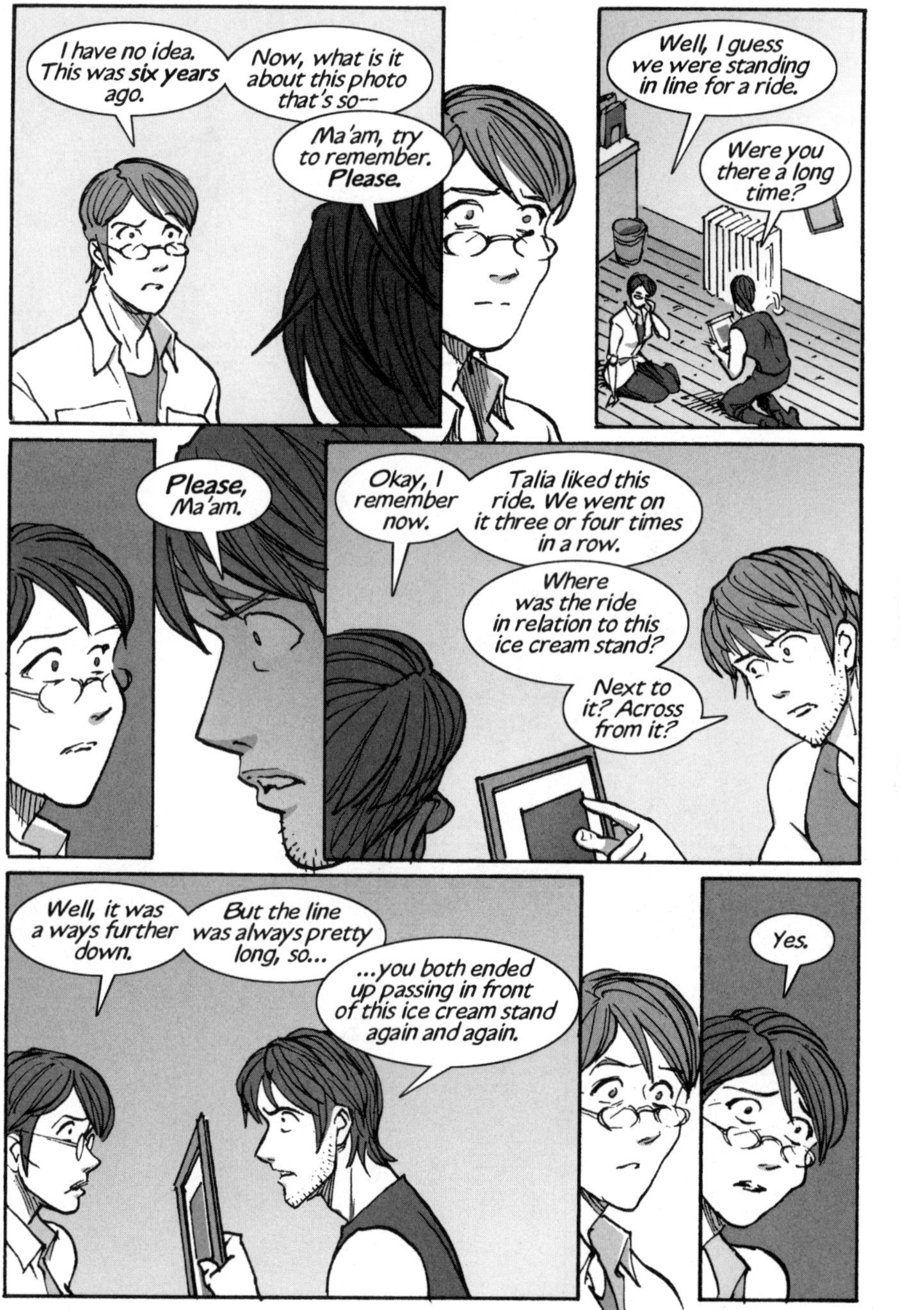
I have no idea. This was **six years** ago.
Now, what is it about this photo that's so--
Ma'am, try to remember. **Please.**
Well, I guess we were standing in line for a ride.
Were you there a long time?
Please, Ma'am.
Okay, I remember now.
Talia liked this ride. We went on it three or four times in a row.
Where was the ride in relation to this ice cream stand?
Next to it? Across from it?
Well, it was a ways further down.
But the line was always pretty long, so...
...you both ended up passing in front of this ice cream stand again and again.
Yes.

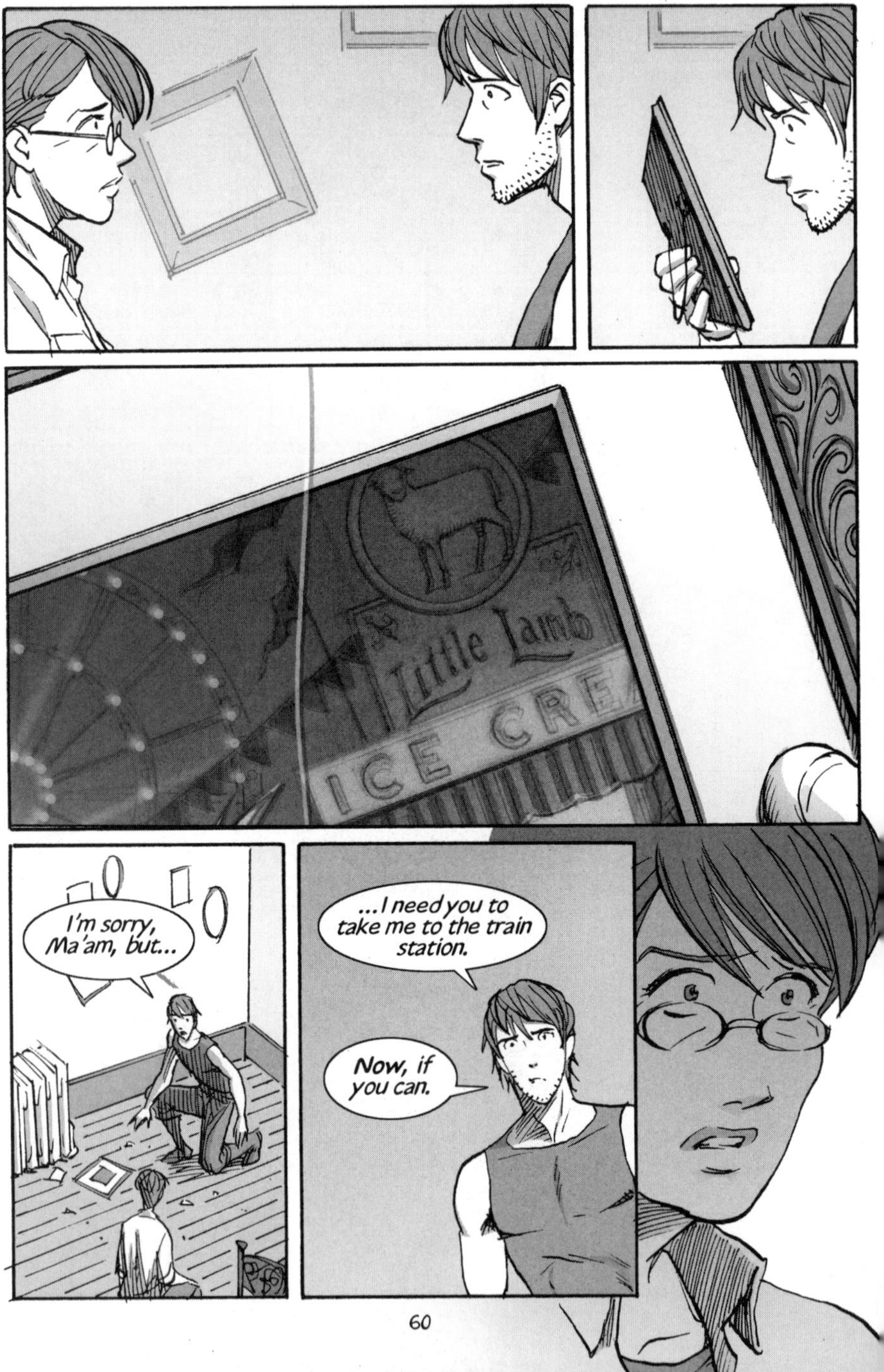
Little Lamb
ICE CRE
I'm sorry, Ma'am, but...
...I need you to take me to the train station.
Now, if you can.

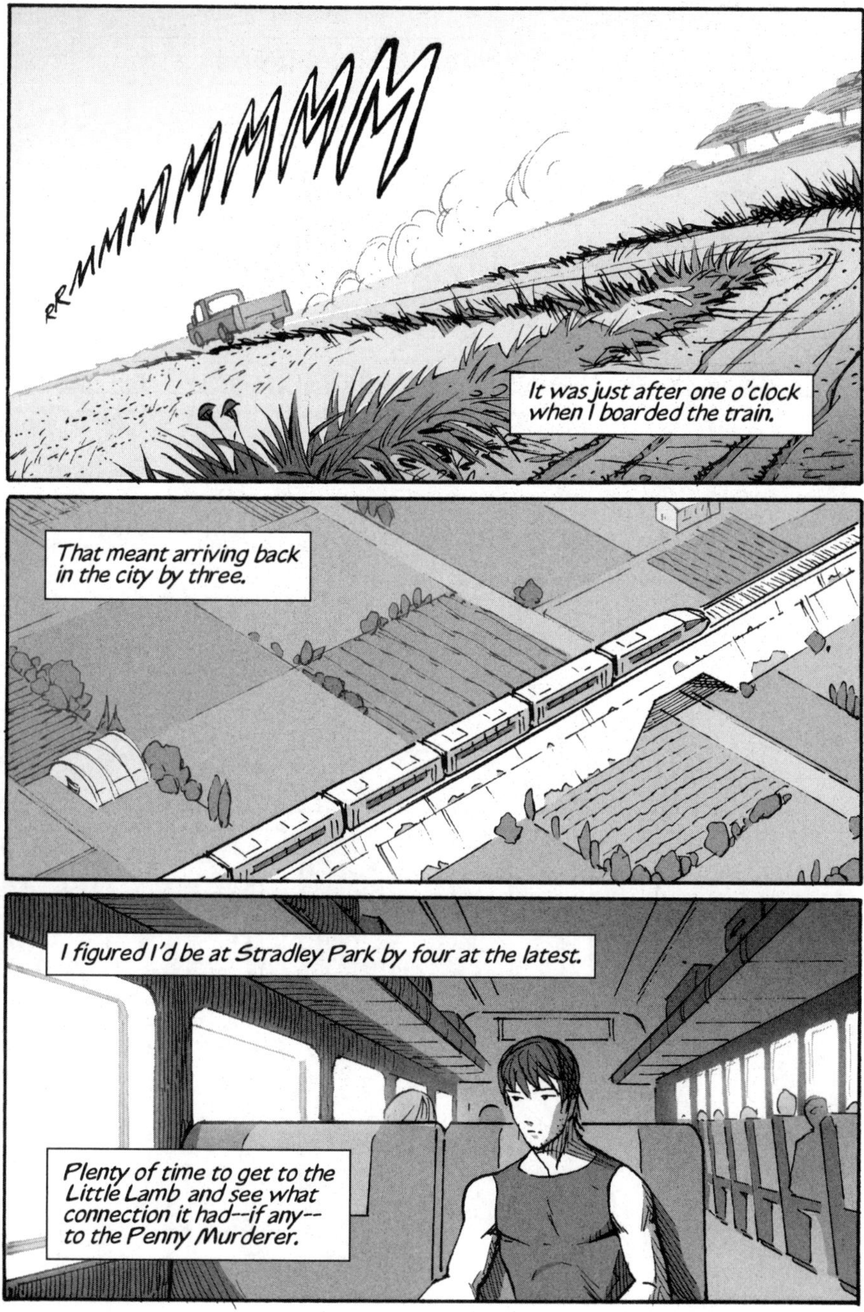
RRMMMMMMMMMM
It was just after one o'clock when I boarded the train.
That meant arriving back in the city by three.
I figured I'd be at Stradley Park by four at the latest.
Plenty of time to get to the Little Lamb and see what connection it had--if any--to the Penny Murderer.

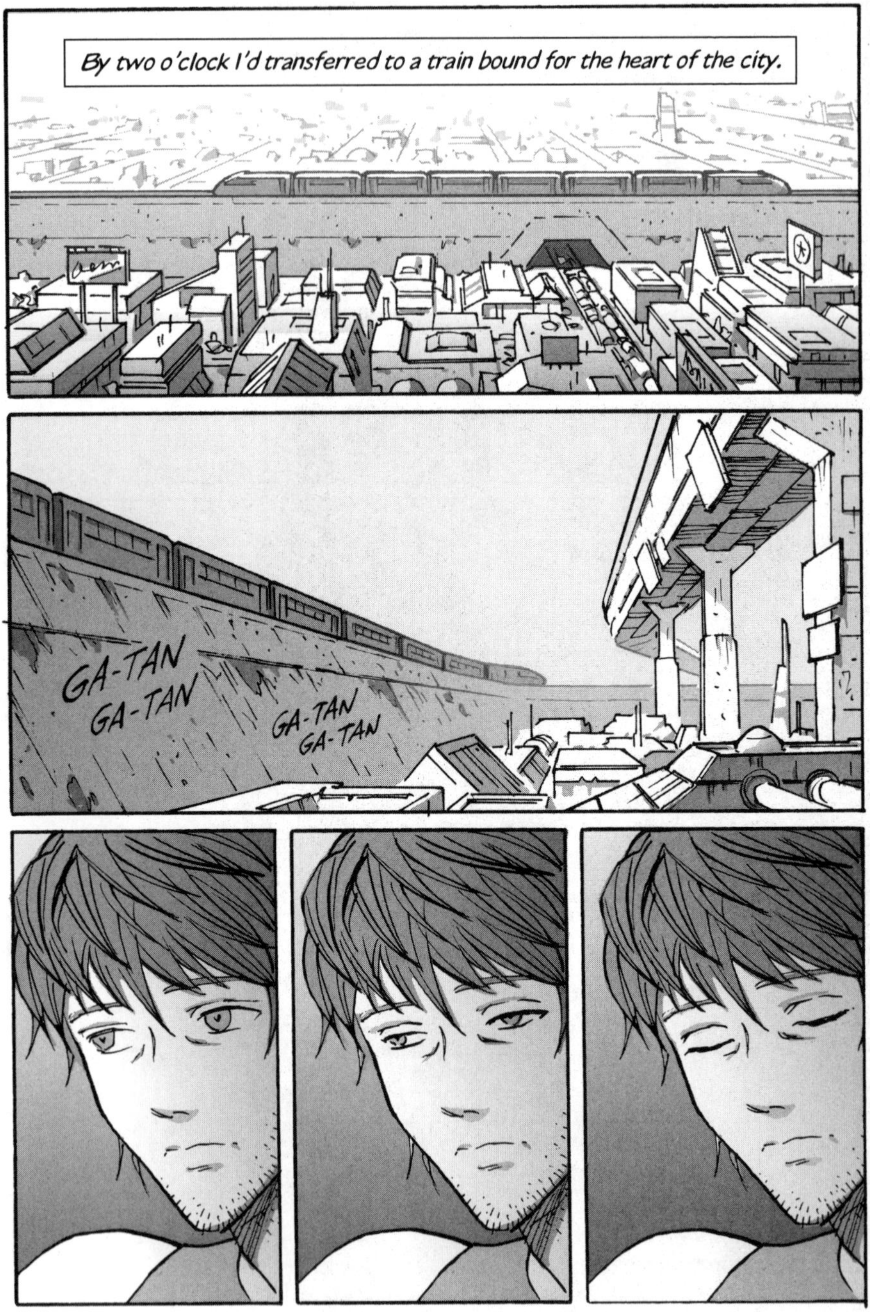
By two o'clock I'd transferred to a train bound for the heart of the city.
GA-TAN
GA-TAN
GA-TAN
GA-TAN

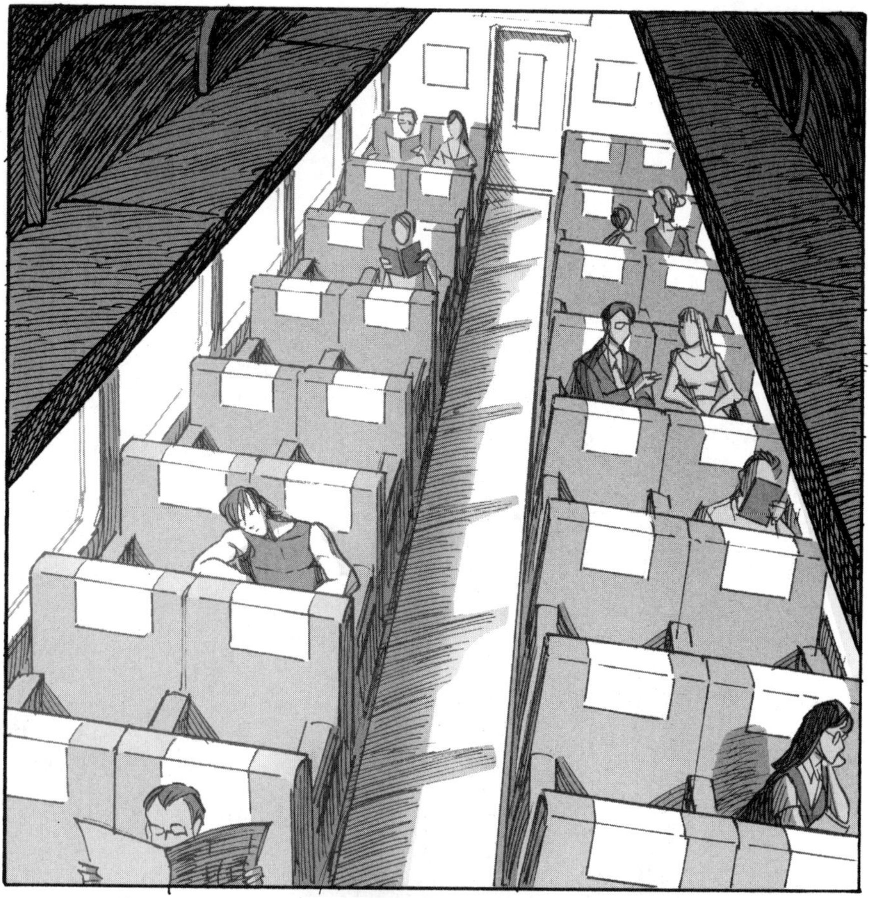

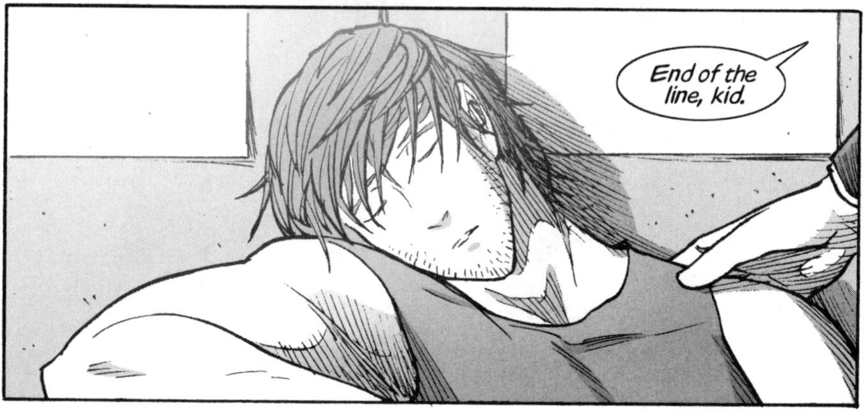
End of the line, kid.

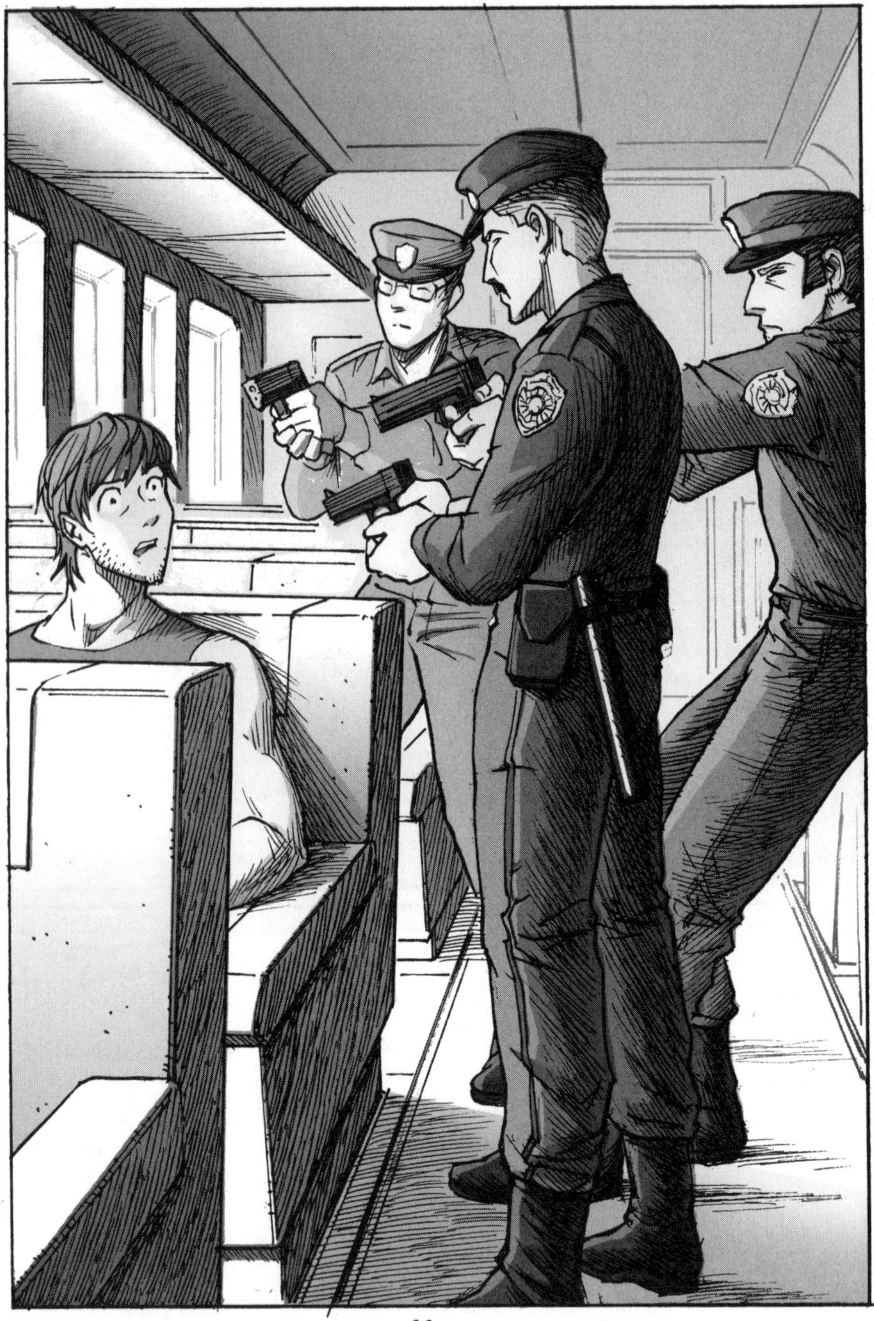

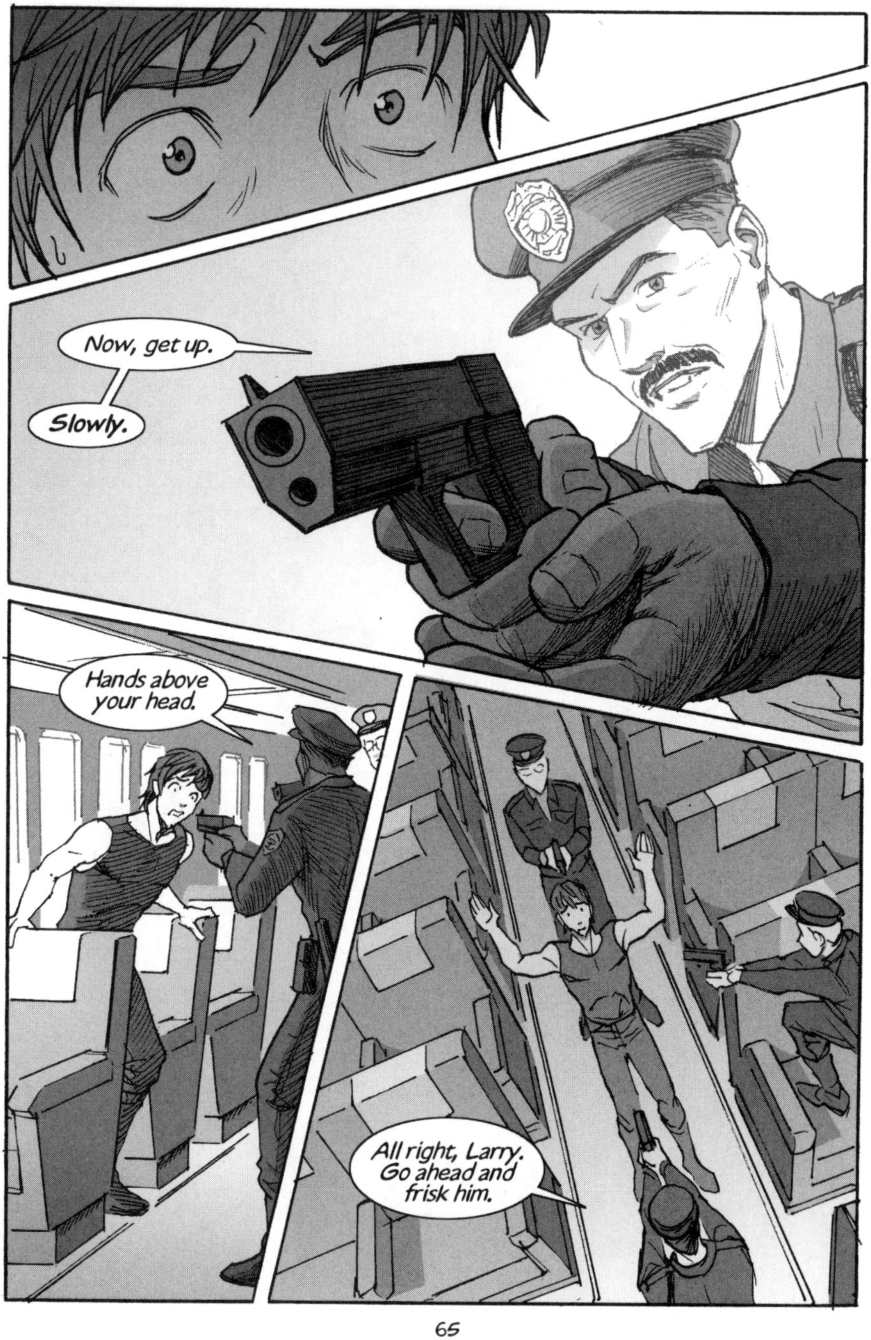
Now, get up.
Slowly.
Hands above your head.
All right, Larry. Go ahead and frisk him.

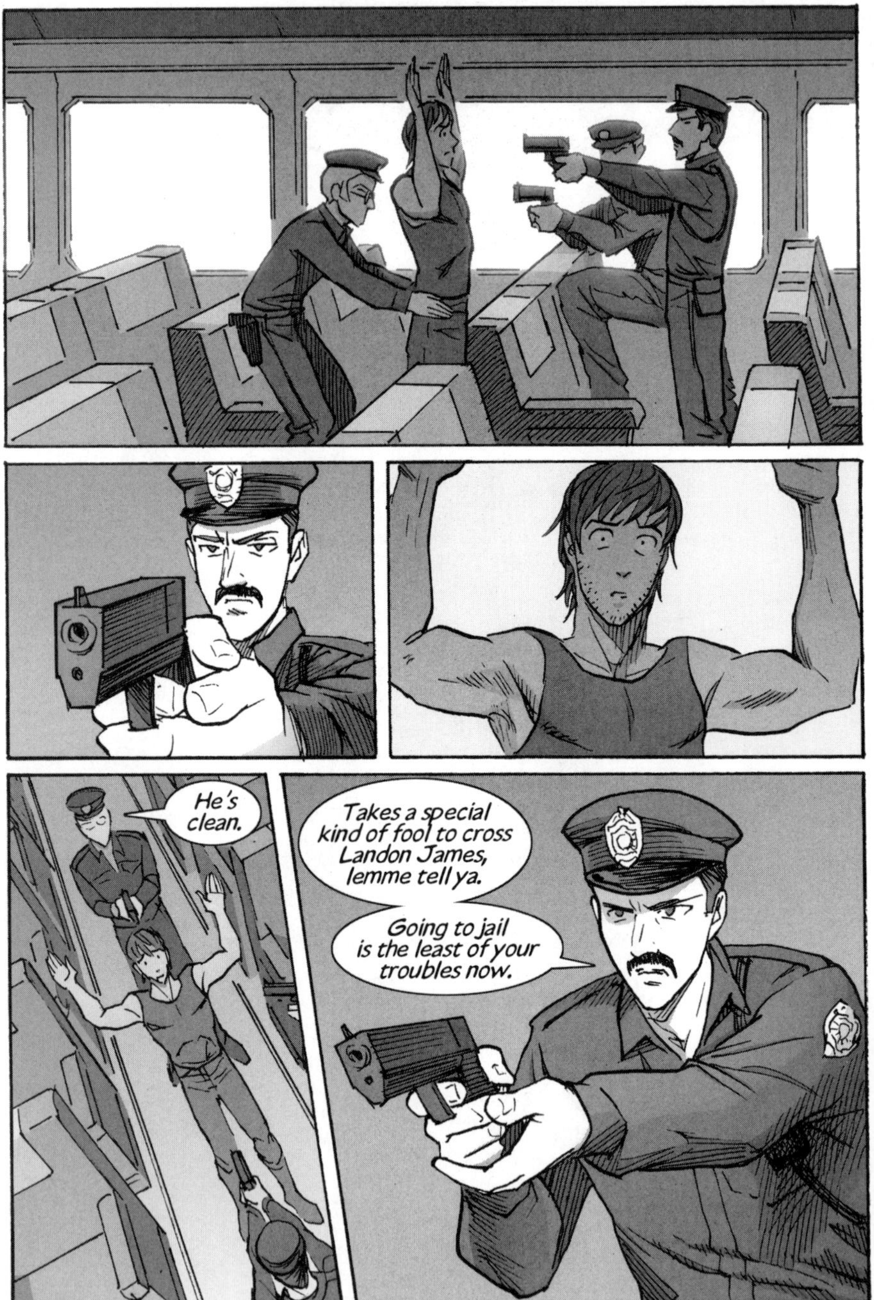
He's clean.
Takes a special kind of fool to cross Landon James, lemme tell ya.
Going to jail is the least of your troubles now.

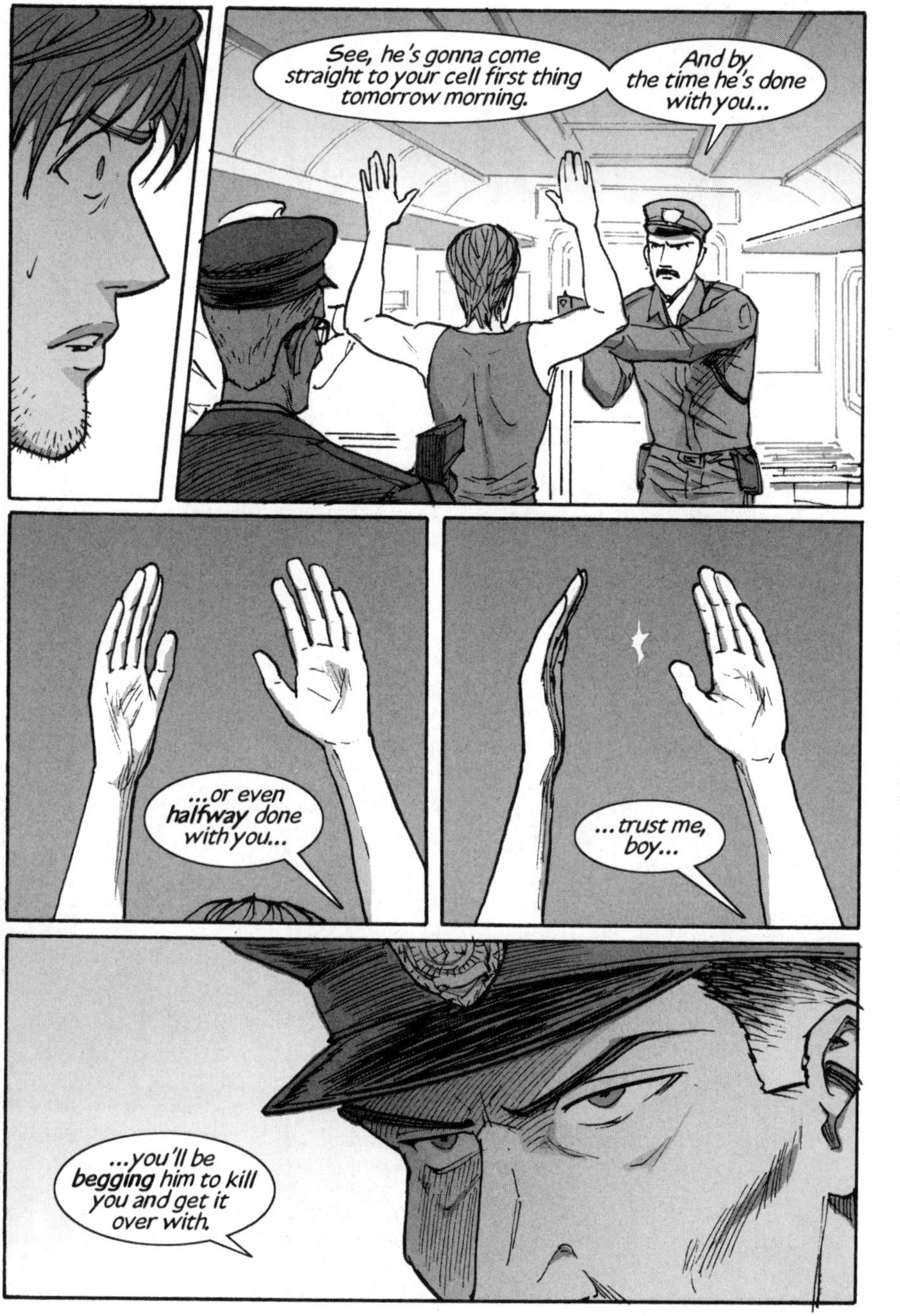
See, he's gonna come straight to your cell first thing tomorrow morning.
And by the time he's done with you...
...or even **halfway** done with you...
...trust me, boy...
...you'll be **begging** him to kill you and get it over with.

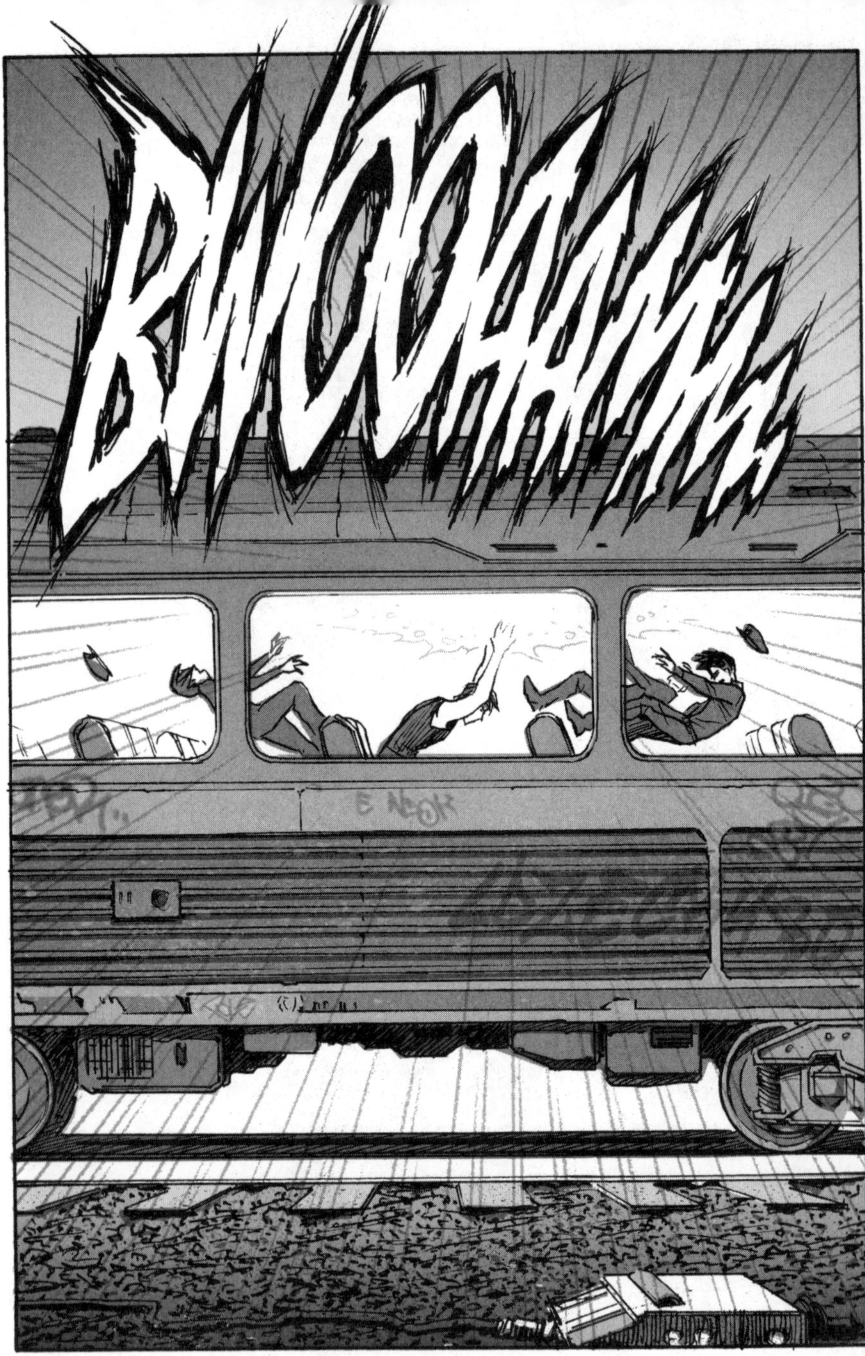

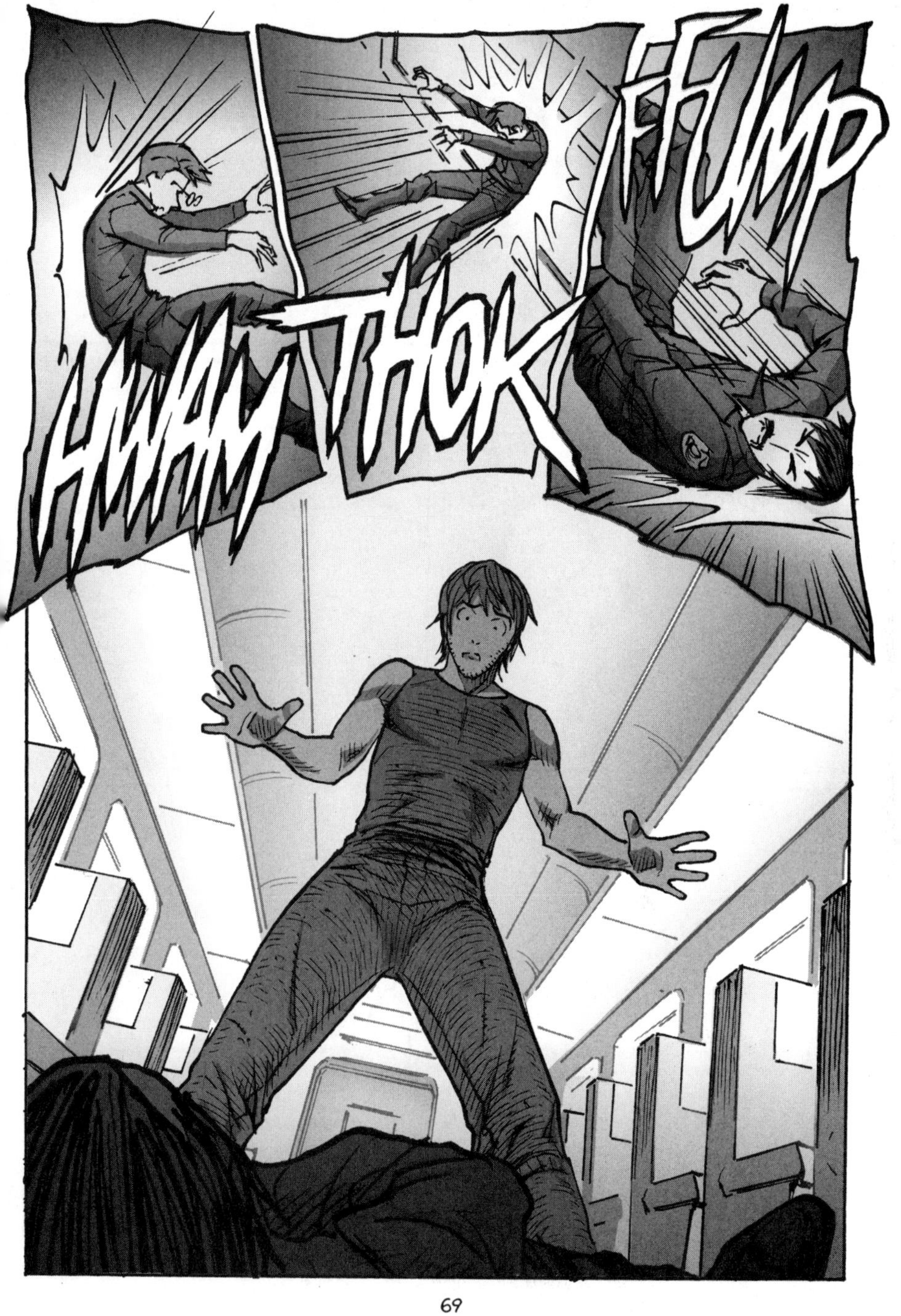
HWAM
THOK
FFUMP

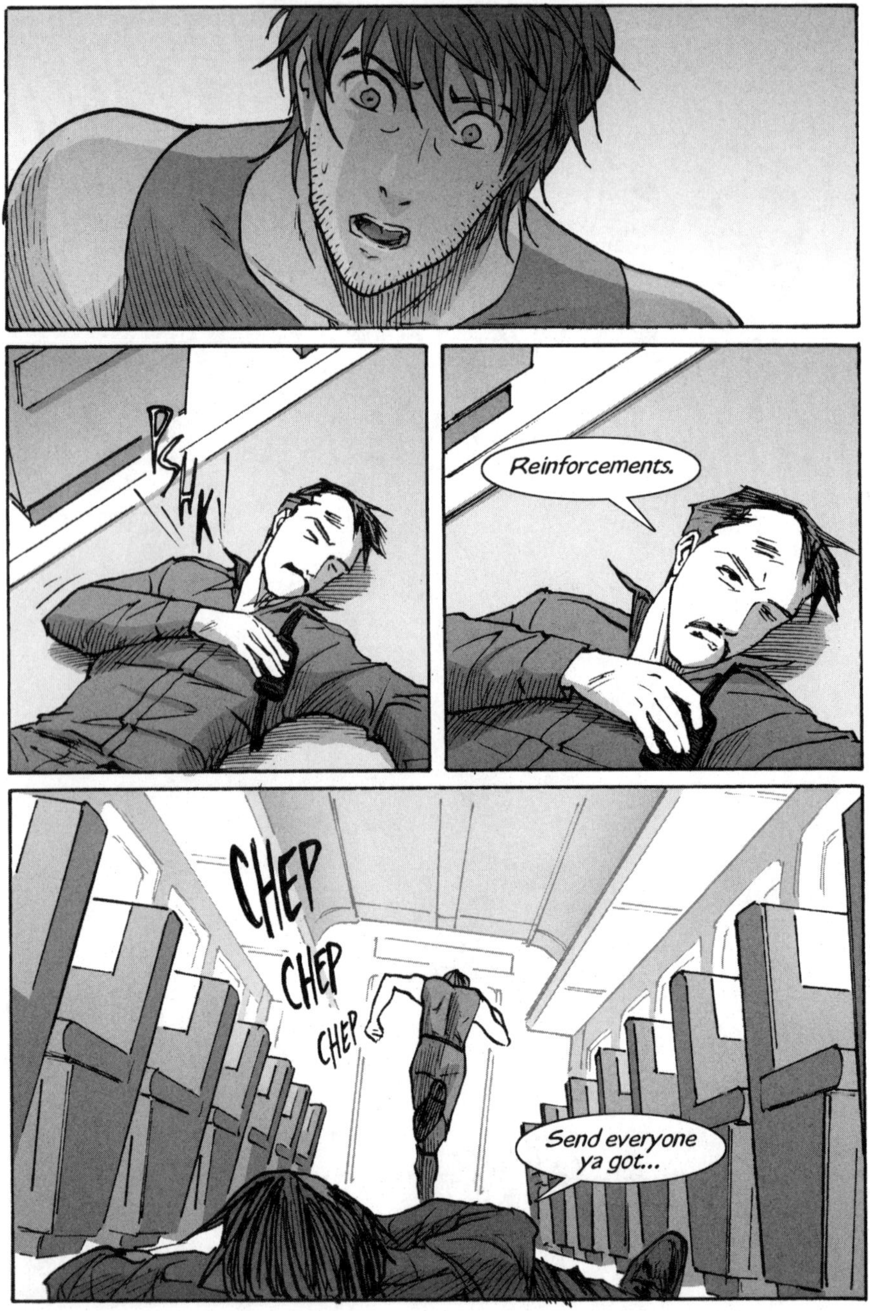
PSHK
Reinforcements.
CHEP
CHEP
CHEP
Send everyone ya got...

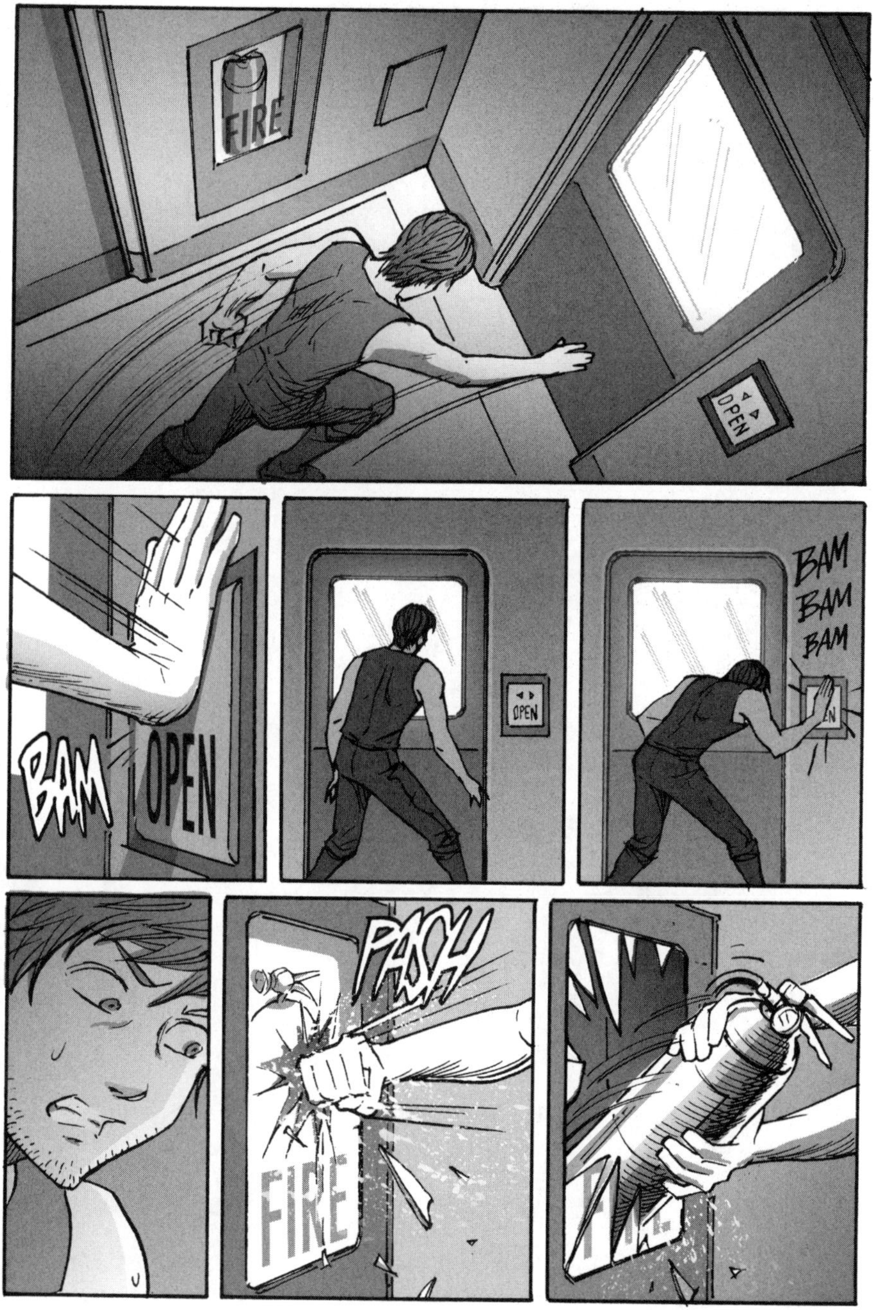
FIRE
OPEN
BAM
OPEN
OPEN
BAM
BAM
BAM
PASSH
FIRE

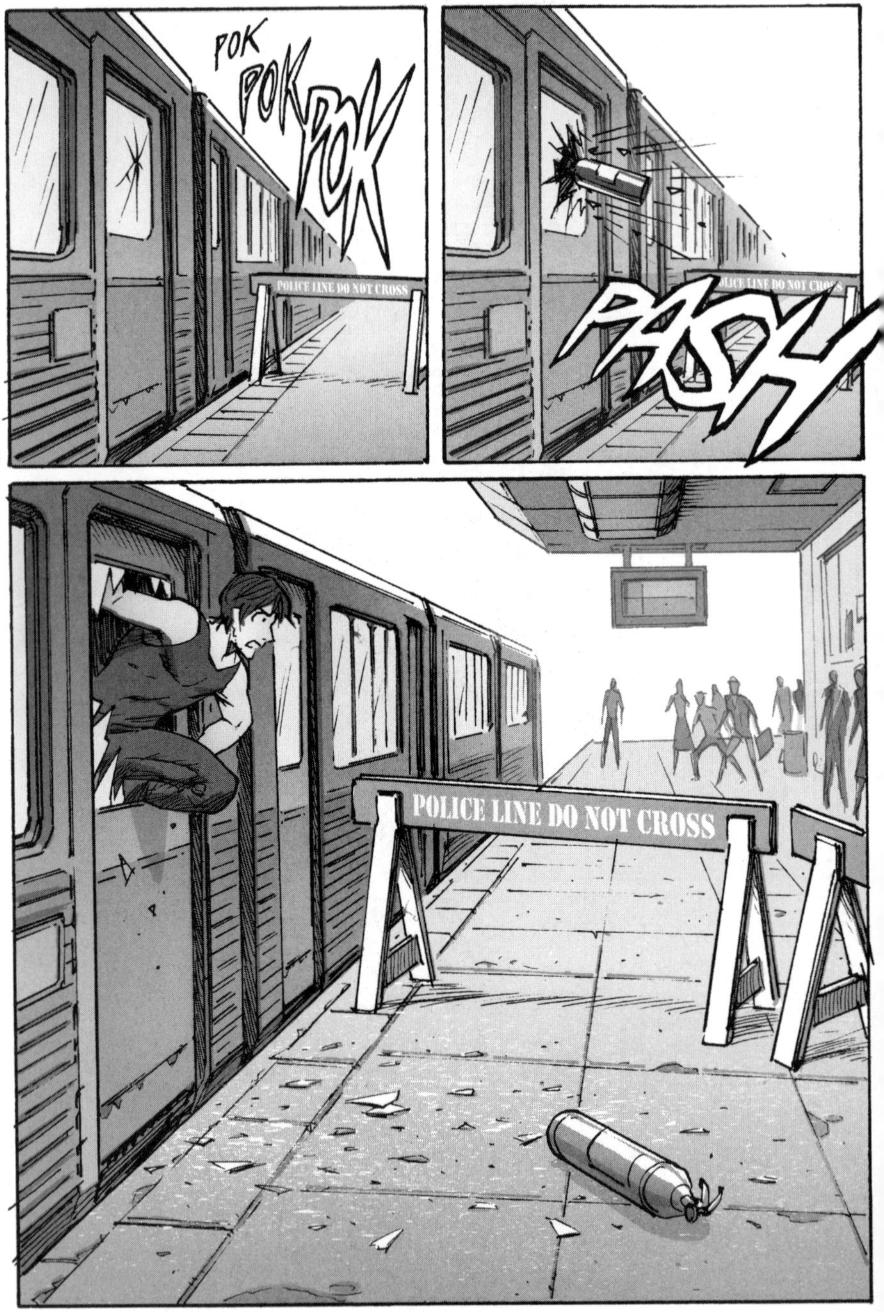
POK
POK POK
POK
POLICE LINE DO NOT CROSS
POLICE LINE DO NOT CROSS
PASH
POLICE LINE DO NOT CROSS

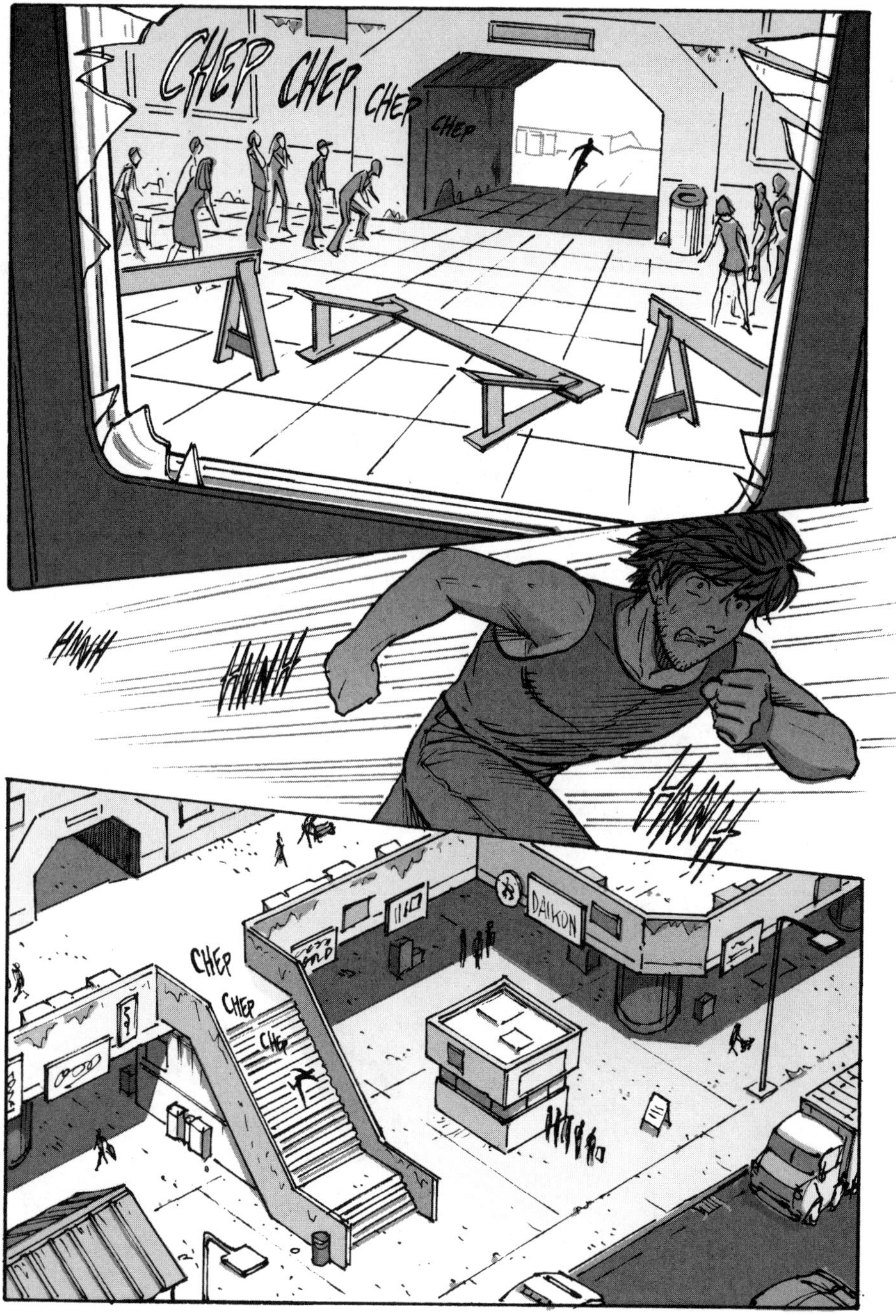
CHEP
CHEP
CHEP
CHEP
HWNH
HWNH
HWNH
DAIKON
CHEP
CHEP
CHEP

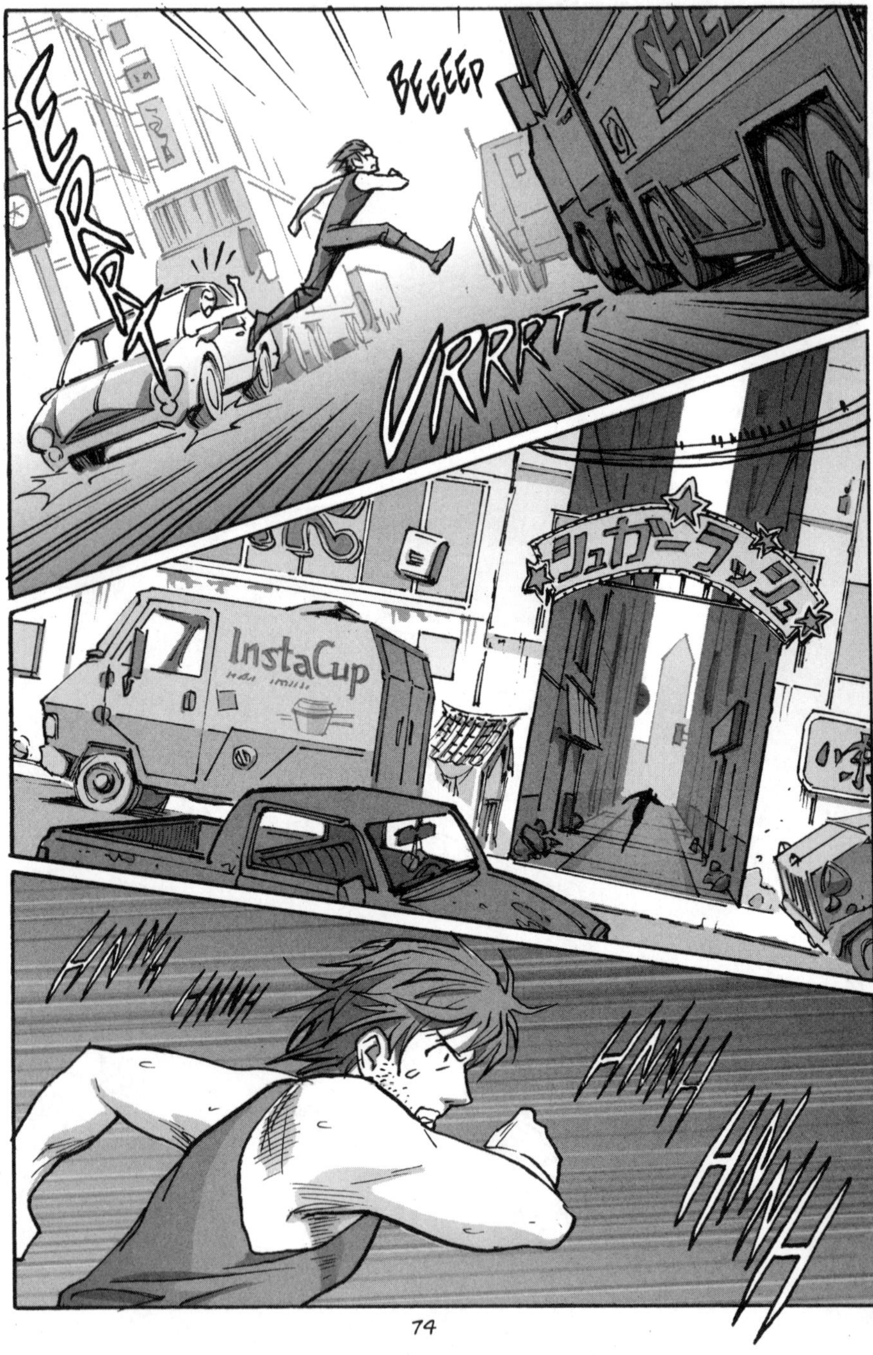
ERRRX
BEEEEP
VRRRTT
シュガーラッシュ
InstaCup
HNNH
HNNH
HNNH
HNNNH

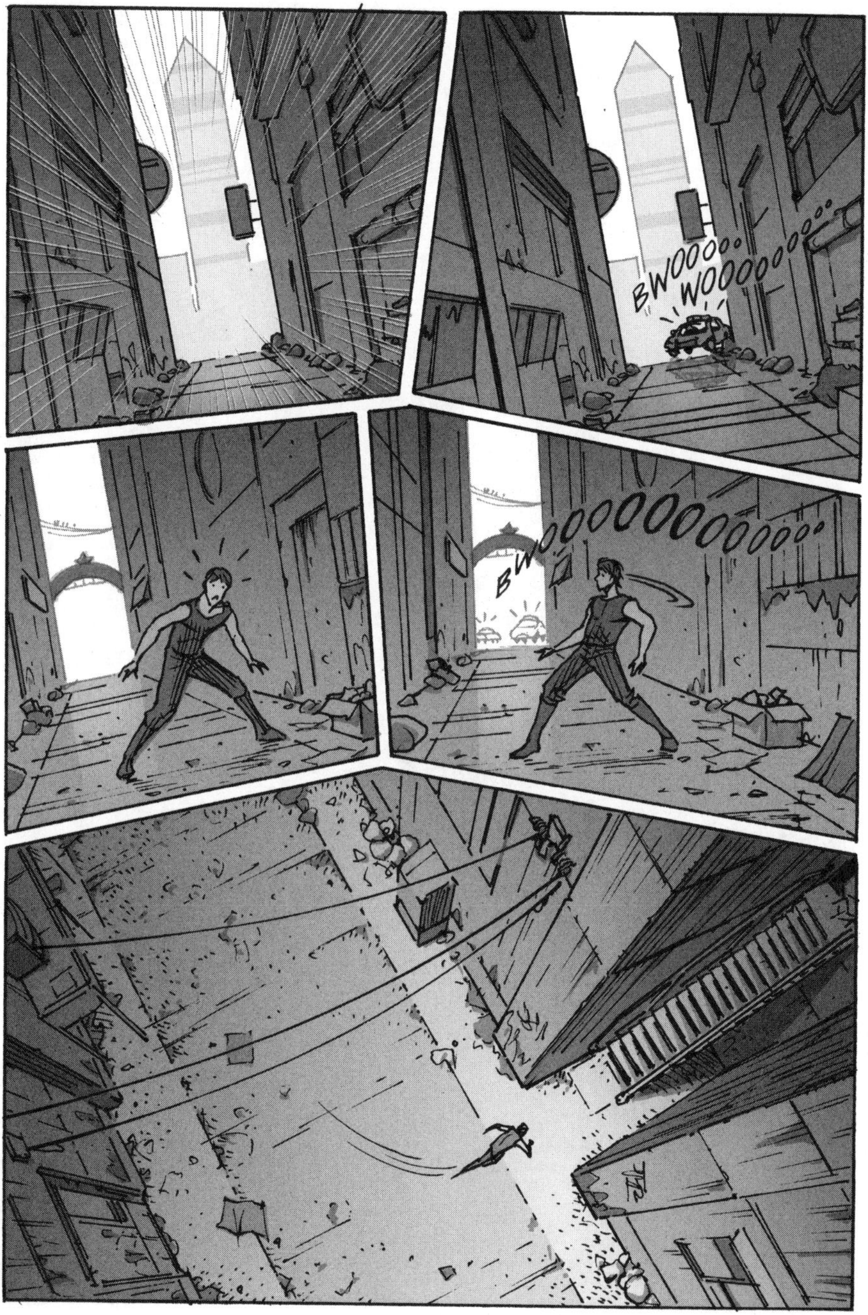
BWOOOOo
WOOOOOOOOoo
BWOOOOOOOOOOOOOOoo

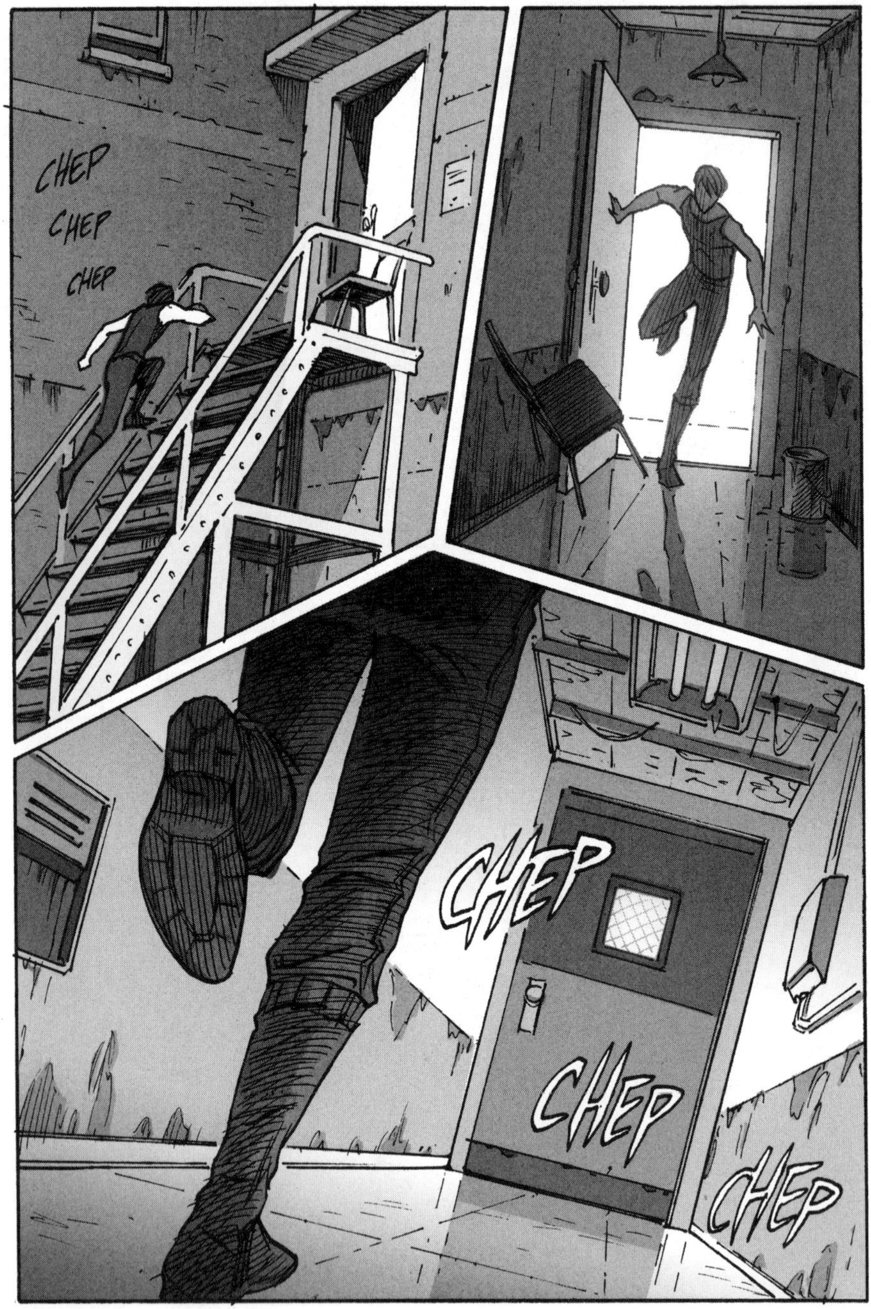
CHEP
CHEP
CHEP
CHEP
CHEP
CHEP

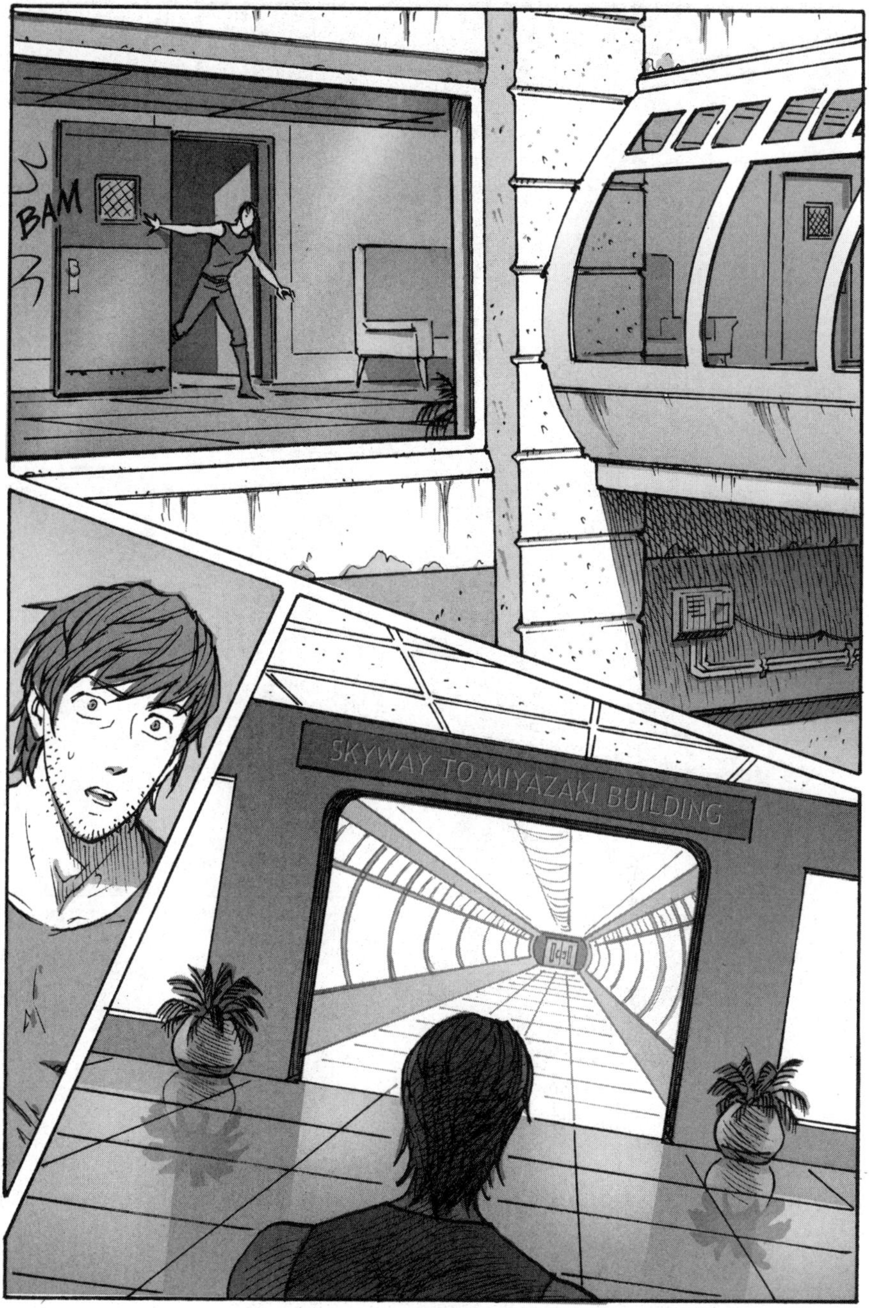
BAM
SKYWAY TO MIYAZAKI BUILDING

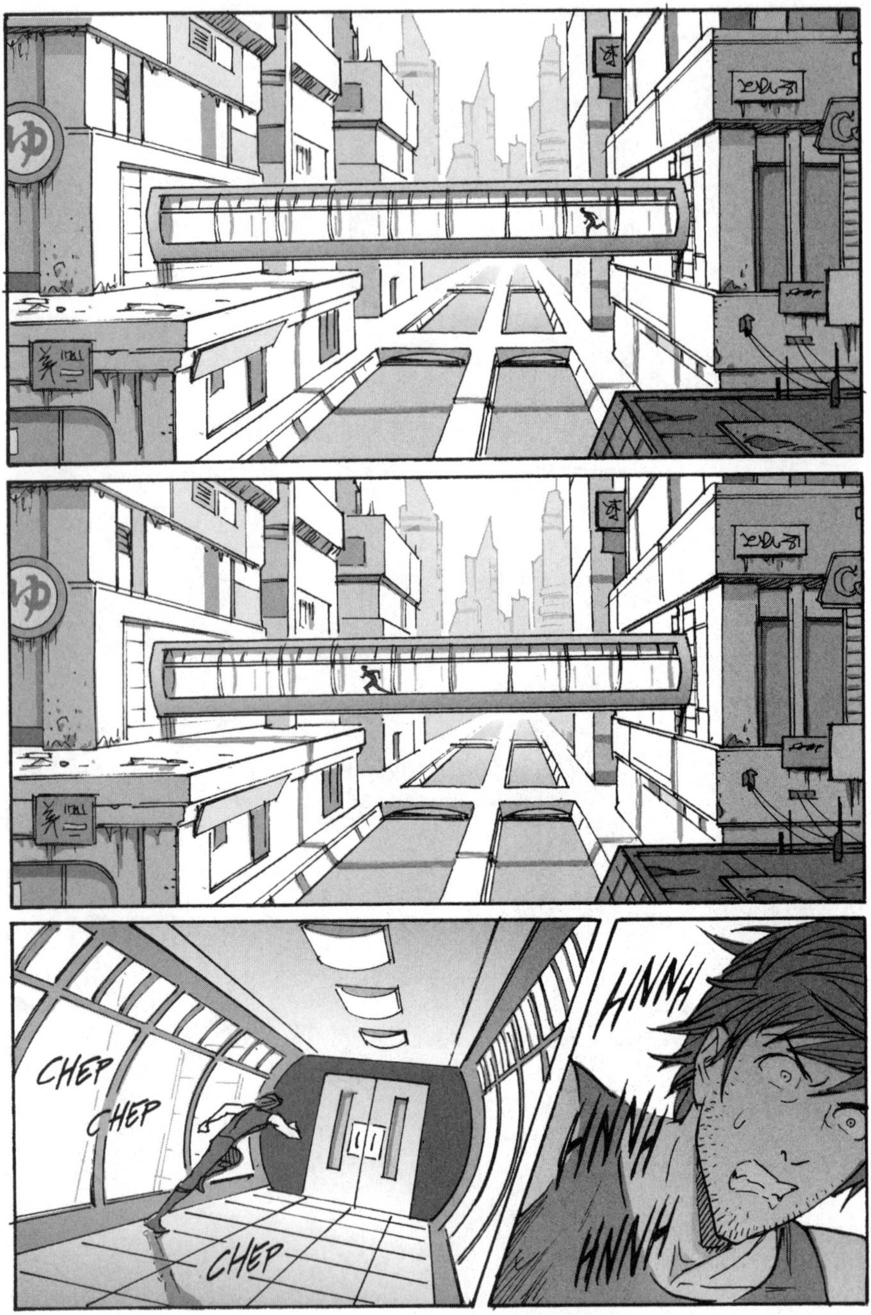
CHEP
CHEP
CHEP
HNNH
HNNH
HNNH

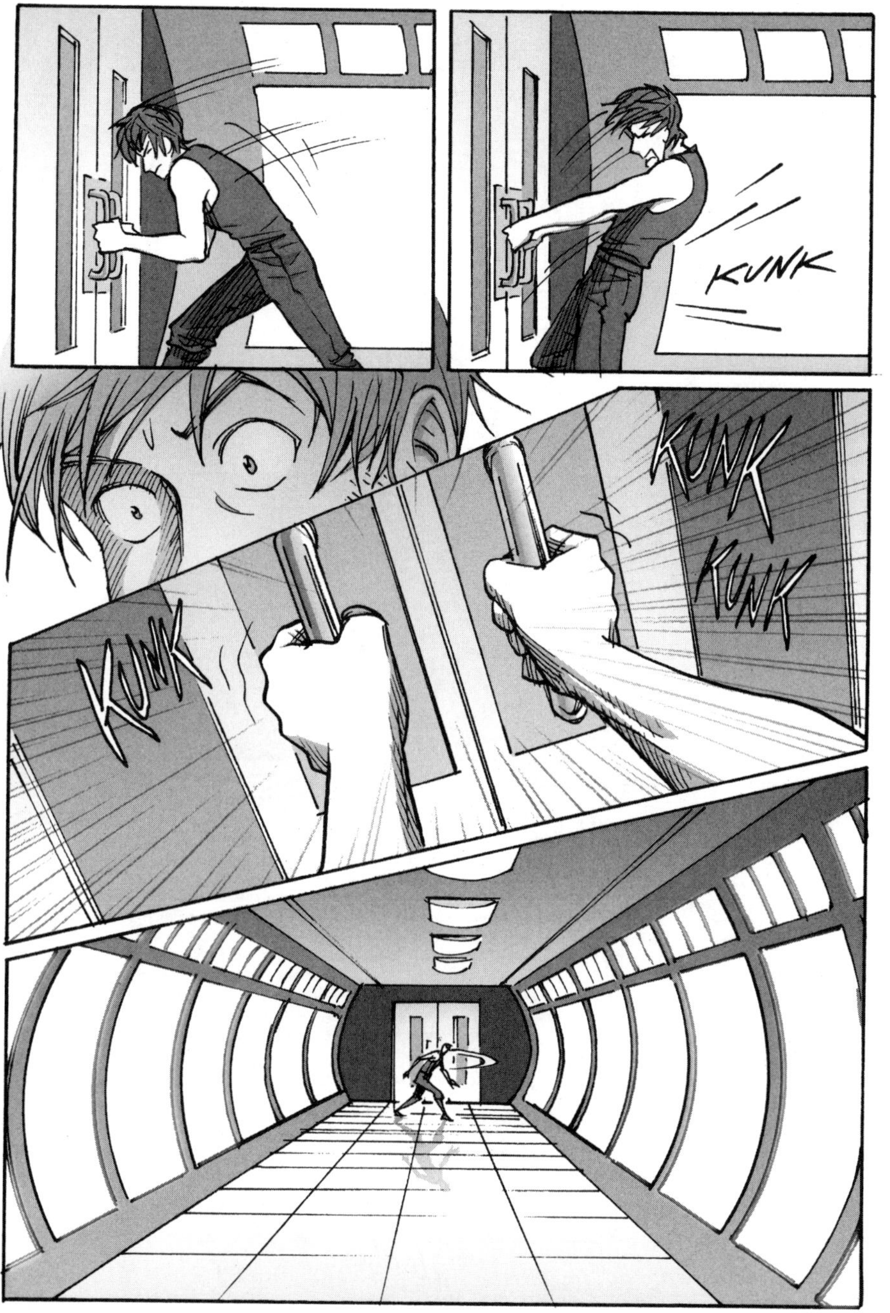
KUNK
KUNK
KUNK
KUNK

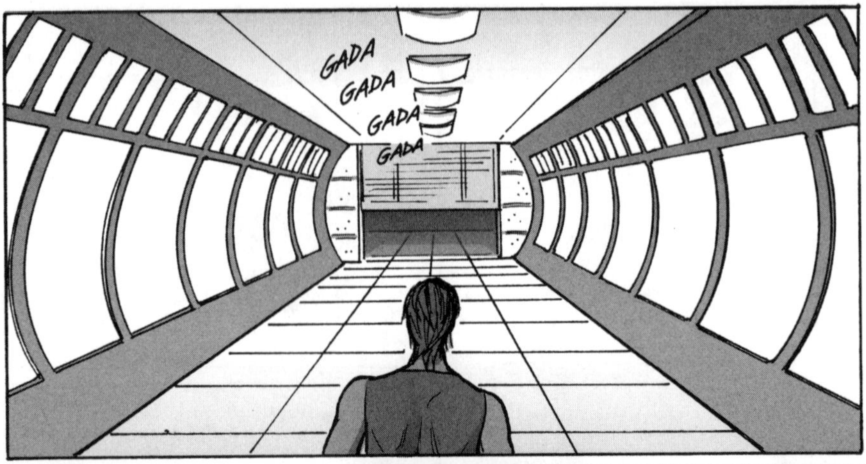
GADA
GADA
GADA
GADA

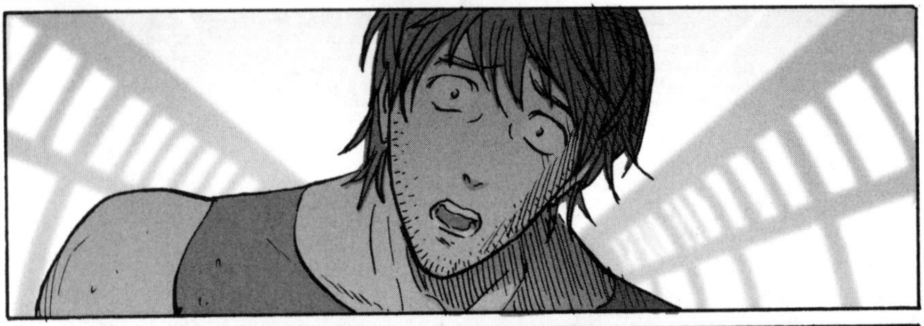

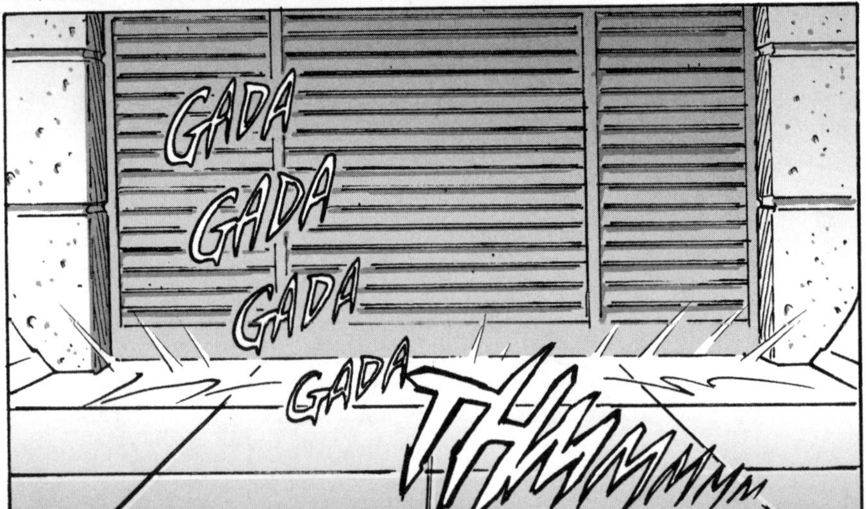
GADA
GADA
GADA
GADA
THMMMMM

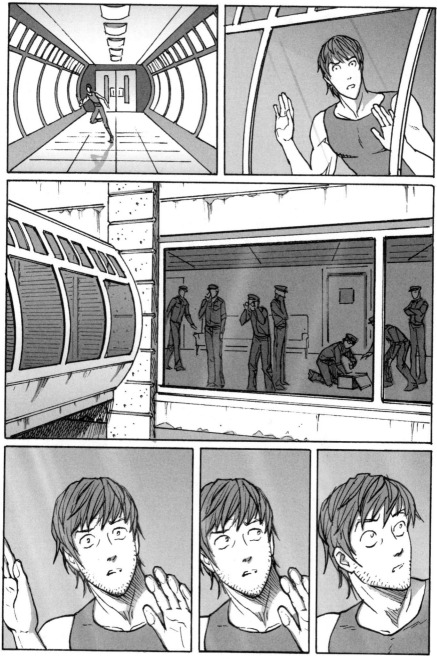

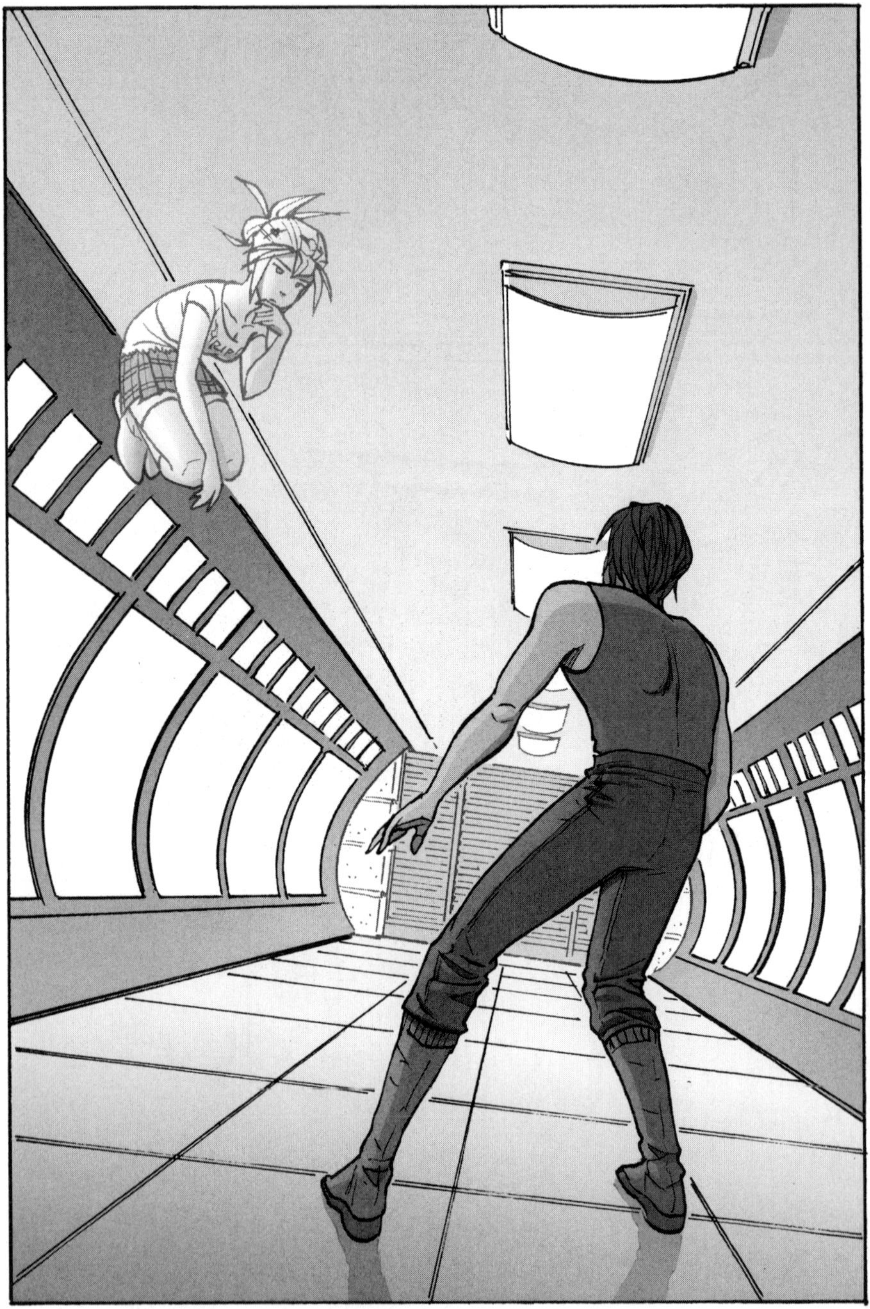

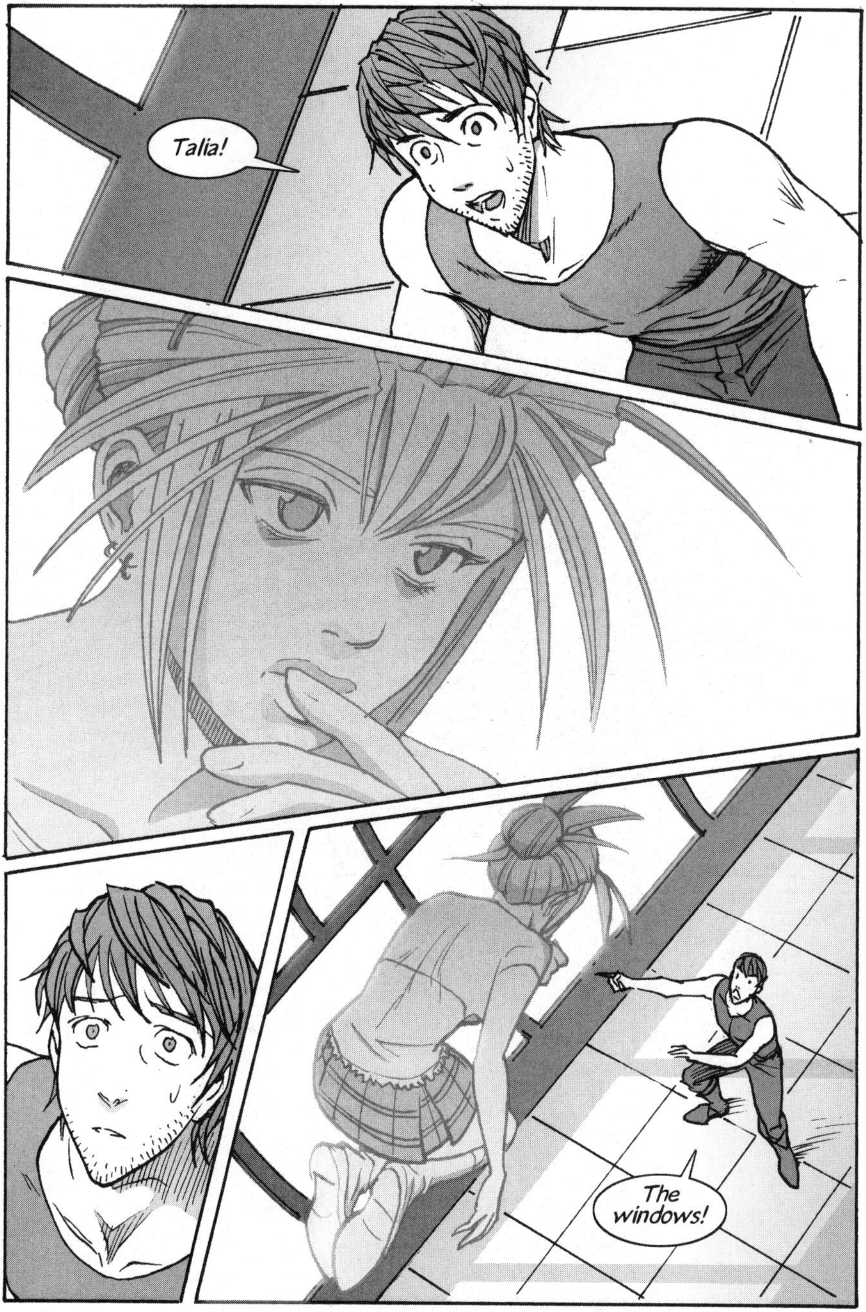
Talia!
The windows!

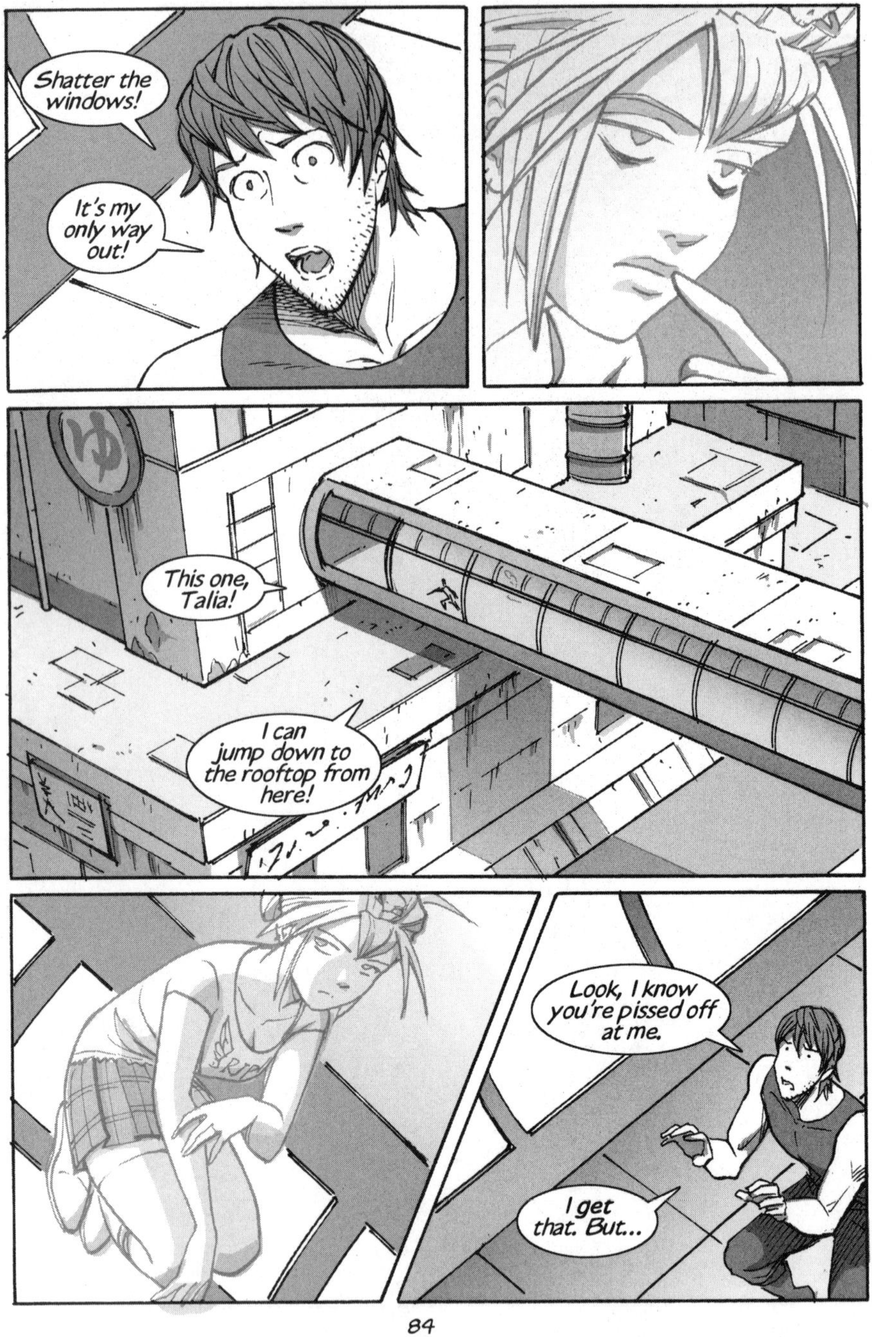
Shatter the windows!
It's my only way out!
This one, Talia!
I can jump down to the rooftop from here!
Look, I know you're pissed off at me.
I get that. But...

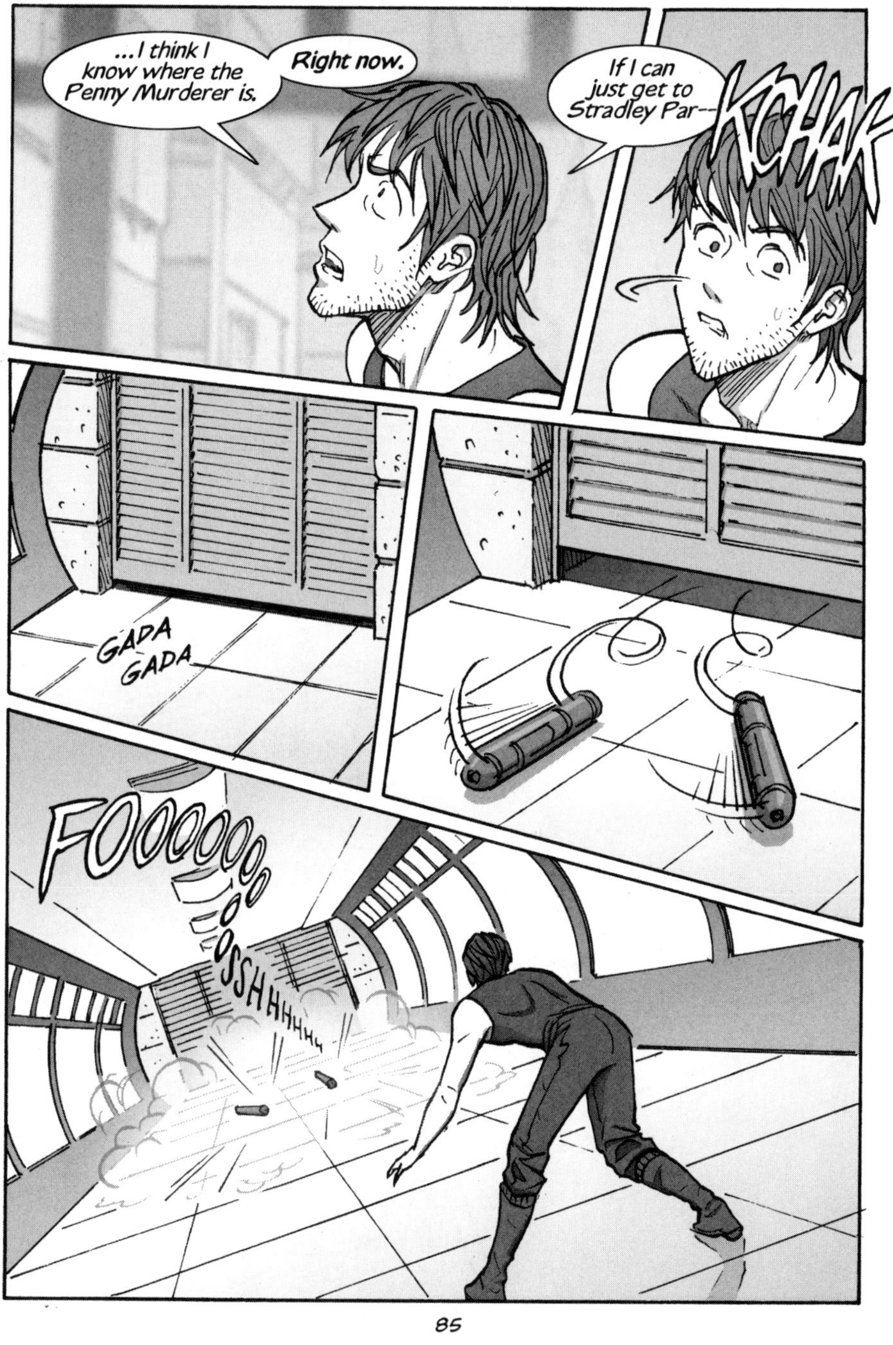
...I think I know where the Penny Murderer is.
Right now.
If I can just get to Stradley Par--
KCHAK
GADA GADA
FOOOOOOOOOOOSSHHHHHH

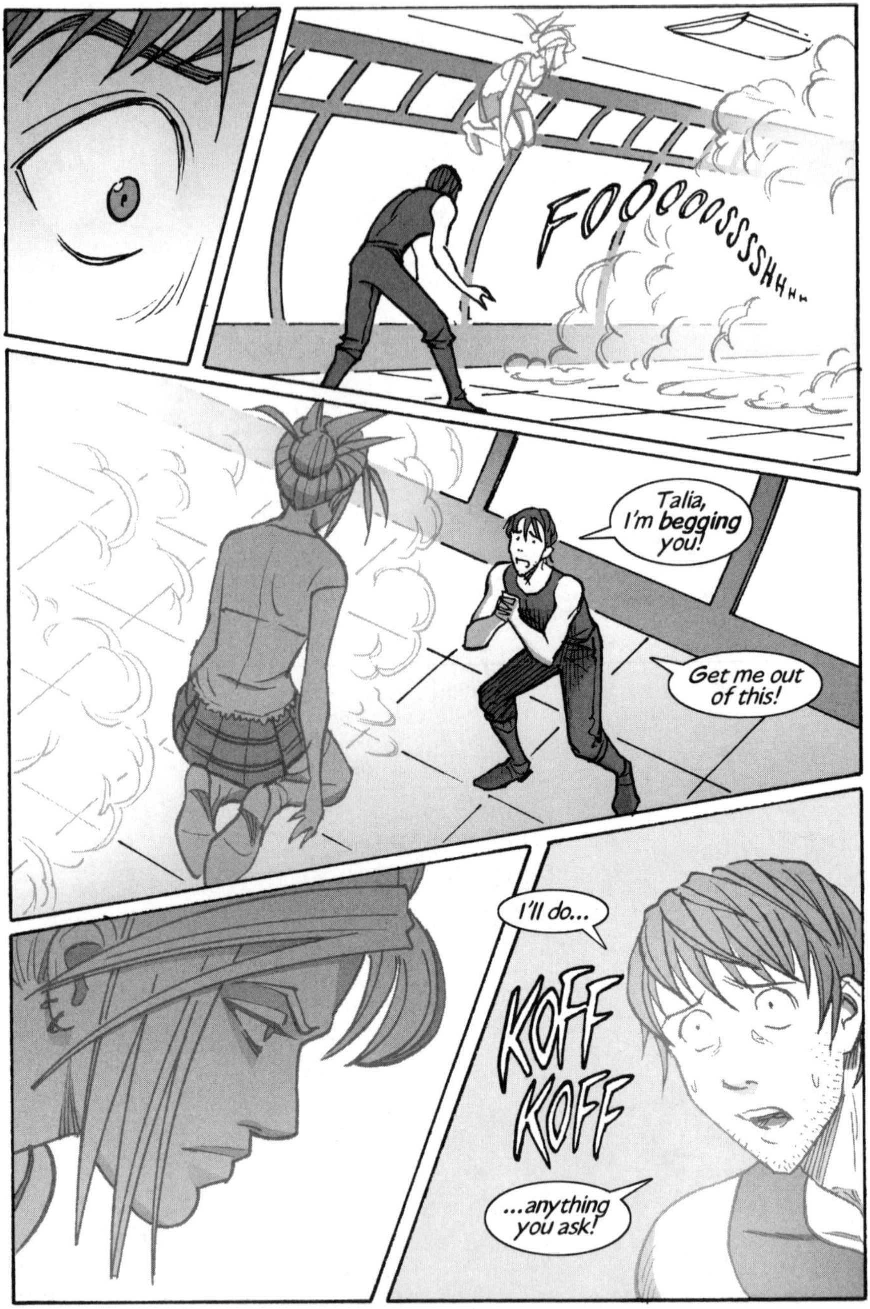
FOOOOOOSSSSHHHH...
Talia, I'm **begging** you!
Get me out of this!
I'll do...
KOFF KOFF
...anything you ask!

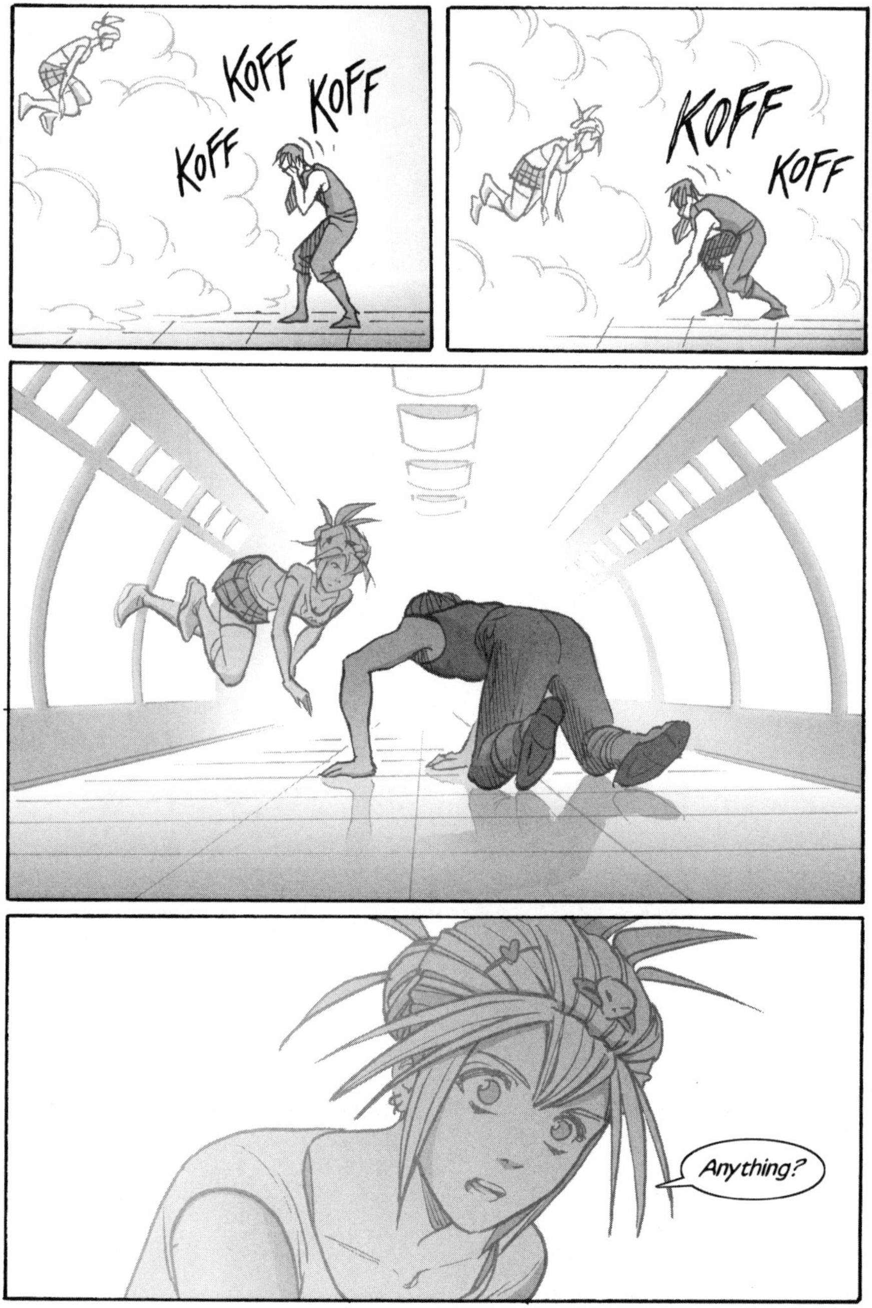
KOFF
KOFF
KOFF
KOFF
KOFF
Anything?

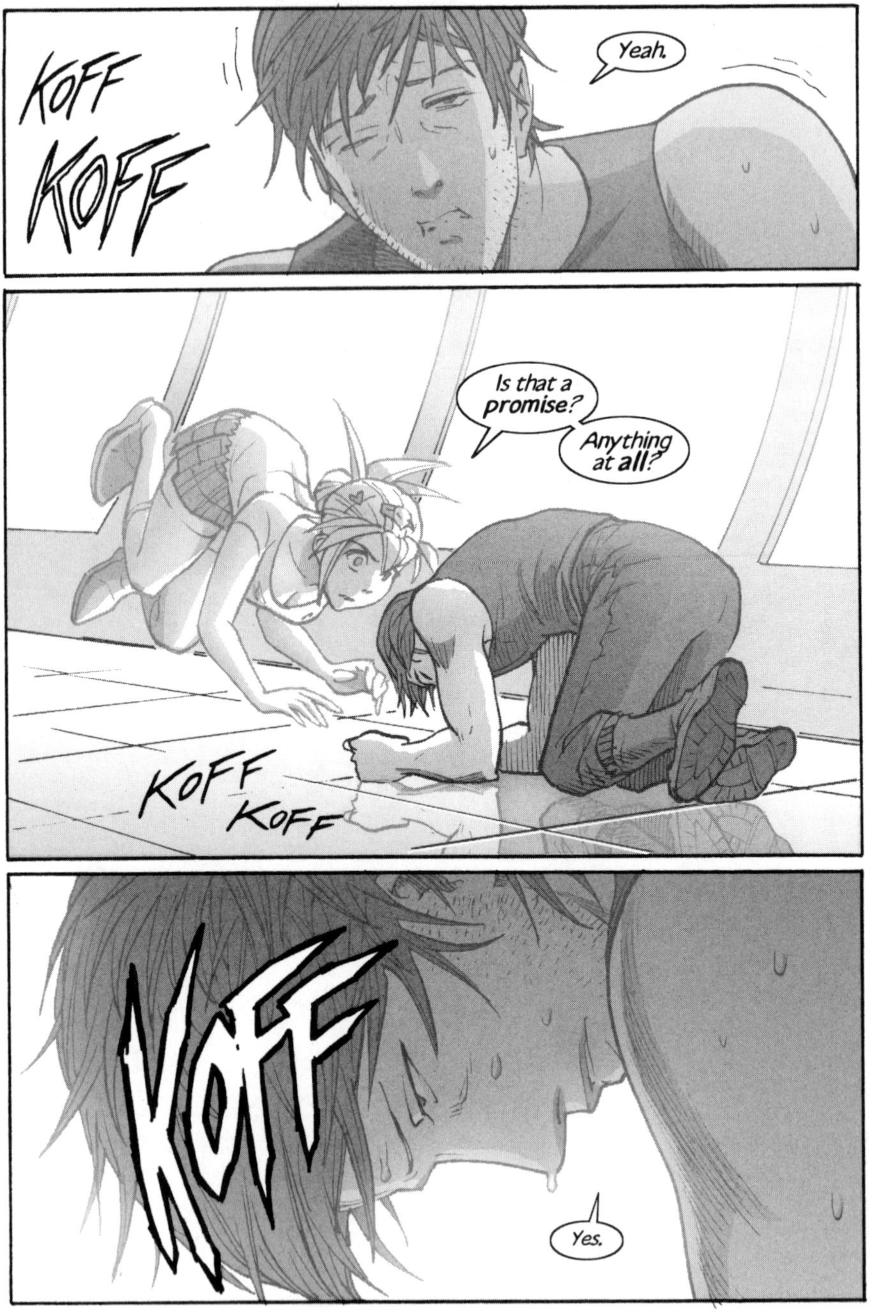
KOFF
KOFF
Yeah.
Is that a promise?
Anything at all?
KOFF
KOFF
KOFF
Yes.

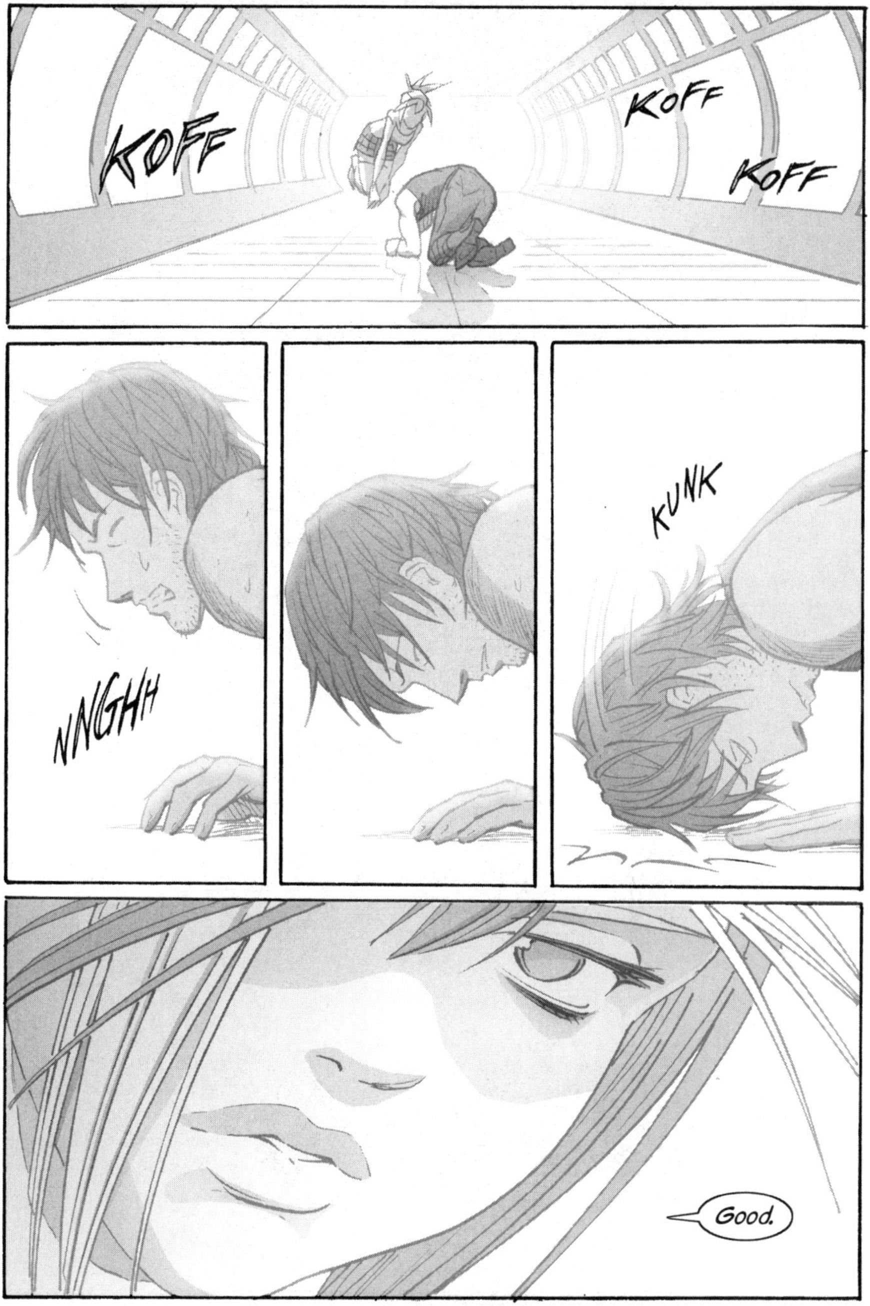
KOFF
KOFF
KOFF
NNGHH
KUNK
Good.

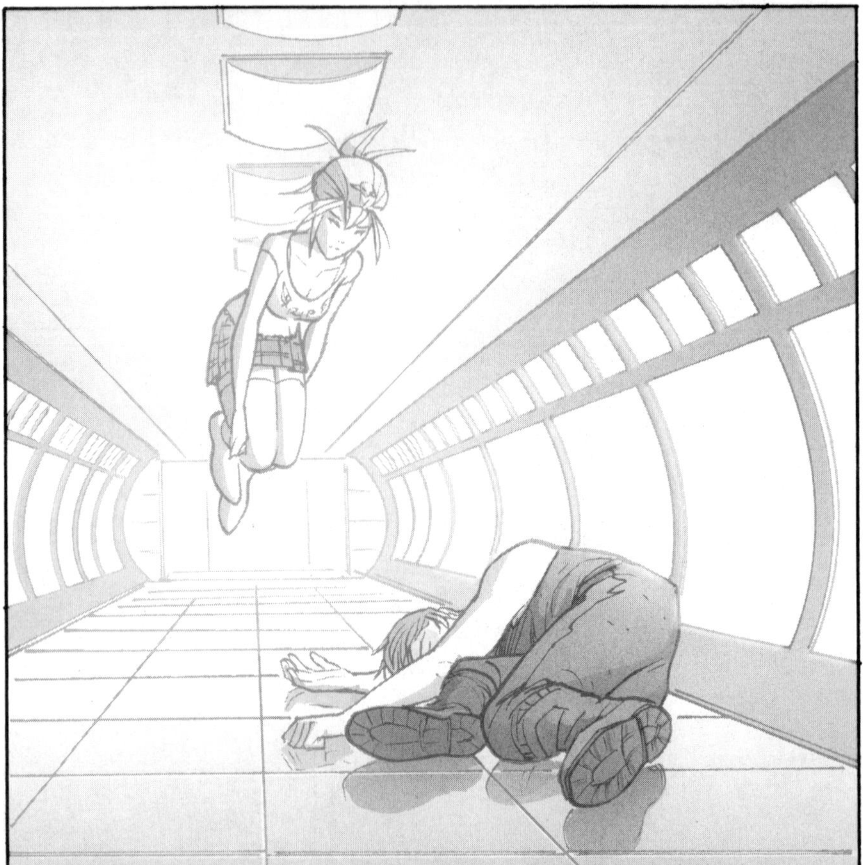

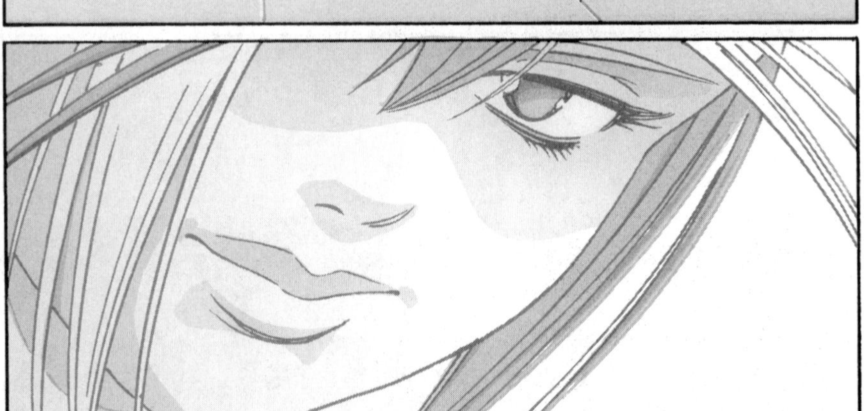

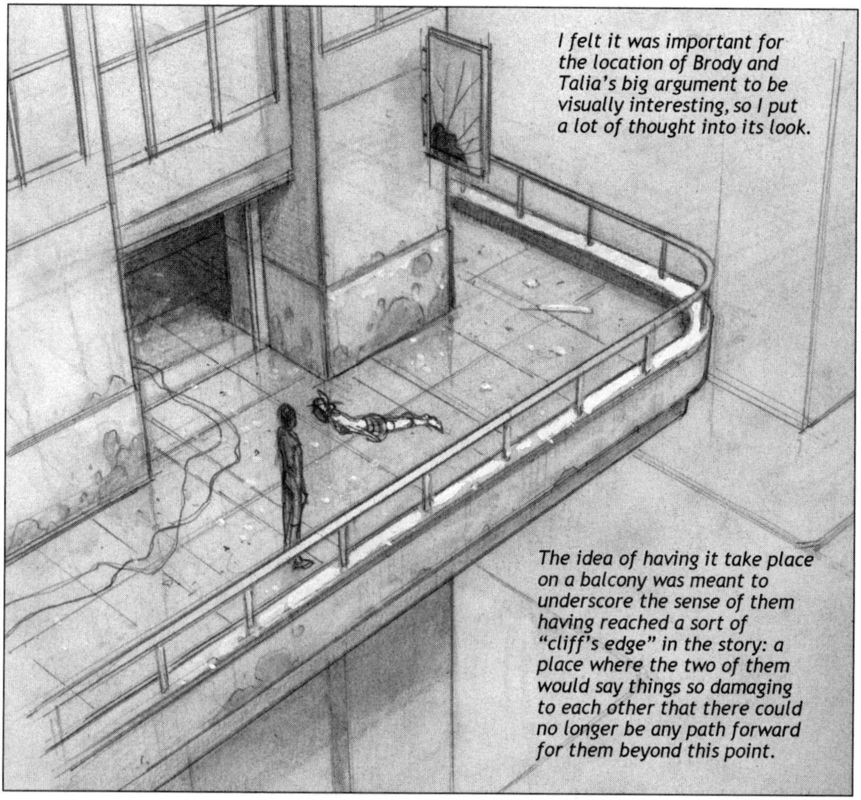

I felt it was important for the location of Brody and Talia's big argument to be visually interesting, so I put a lot of thought into its look.

The idea of having it take place on a balcony was meant to underscore the sense of them having reached a sort of "cliff's edge" in the story: a place where the two of them would say things so damaging to each other that there could no longer be any path forward for them beyond this point.

Designing Talia's mother was a bit of a challenge. Making her simply look like an older version of Talia seemed completely wrong, so I chose instead to focus on her backstory and attempt to convey some of it by way of her appearance.

I saw her as person made stronger by the tragedies she had suffered through. Giving her glasses was a sort of playful twist on how clear-sighted she is as a character. Her eyes see everything, especially when it comes to people trying to deceive her.

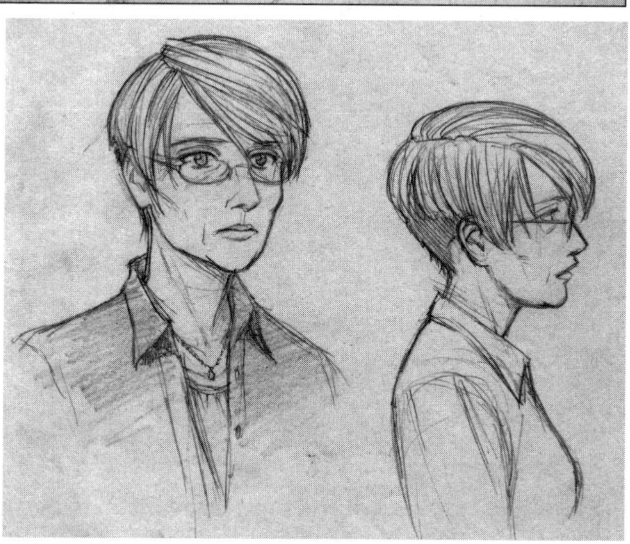

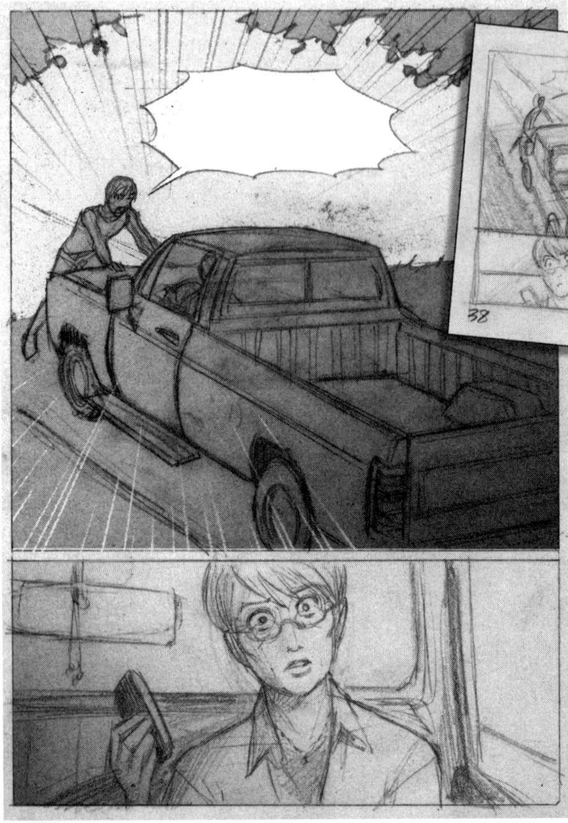

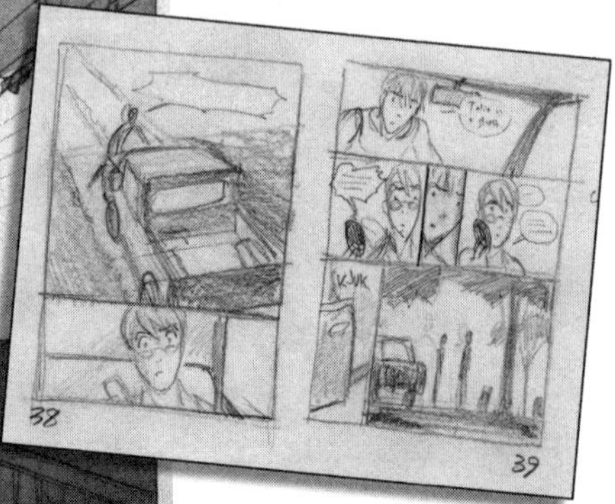

For the scene in which Brody blurts out the truth to Talia's mother I'd originally planned a sort of crane shot, believing that an elevated point of view would enhance the drama of this pivotal moment.

Over time, though, I decided it just wasn't working. I was going "big" and straining to maximize the excitement, but somehow distancing the reader from what was happening and getting an oddly low-key effect. In the end I felt we needed to be closer in on Brody, joining him at his side and sharing his panic as he went for broke.

I also added two more silent panels to build extra tension as the reader waits to see how Talia's mother will react.

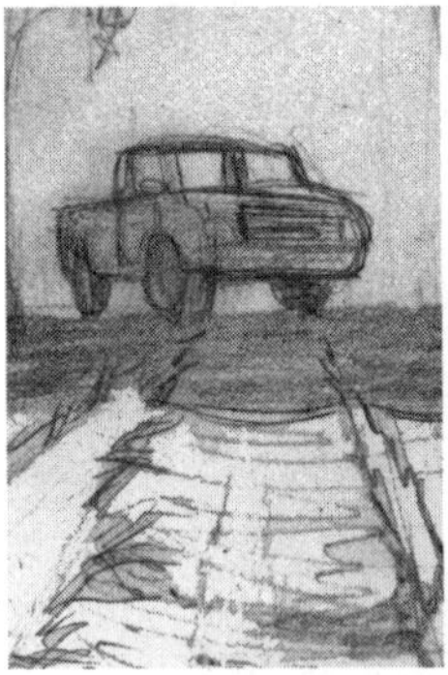

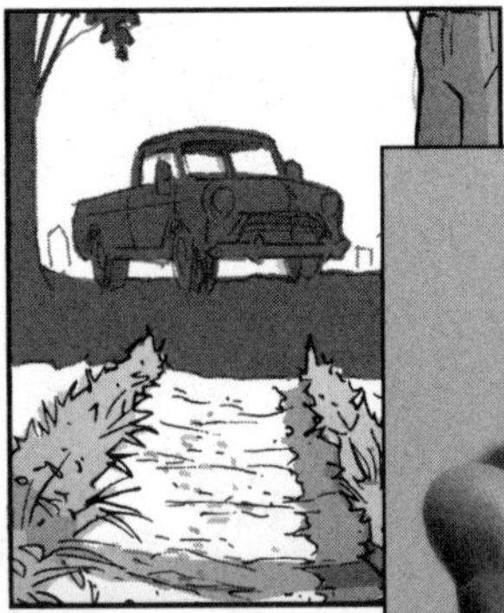

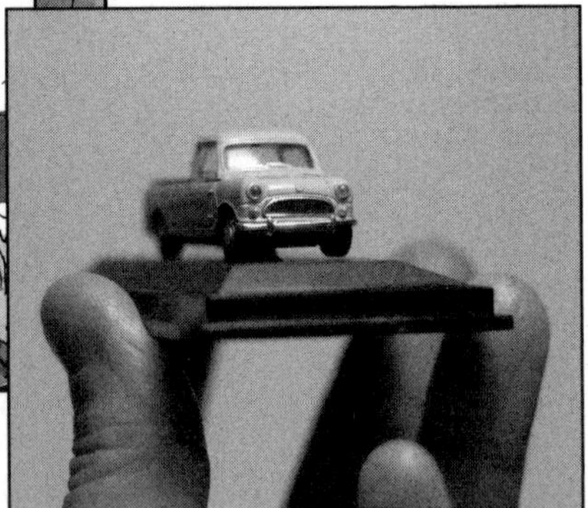

To help with drawing the truck I bought a cheap plastic model truck at a dollar store. It was great for getting the basic shape right, though I did have to add side mirrors, since the model had omitted them for some reason.

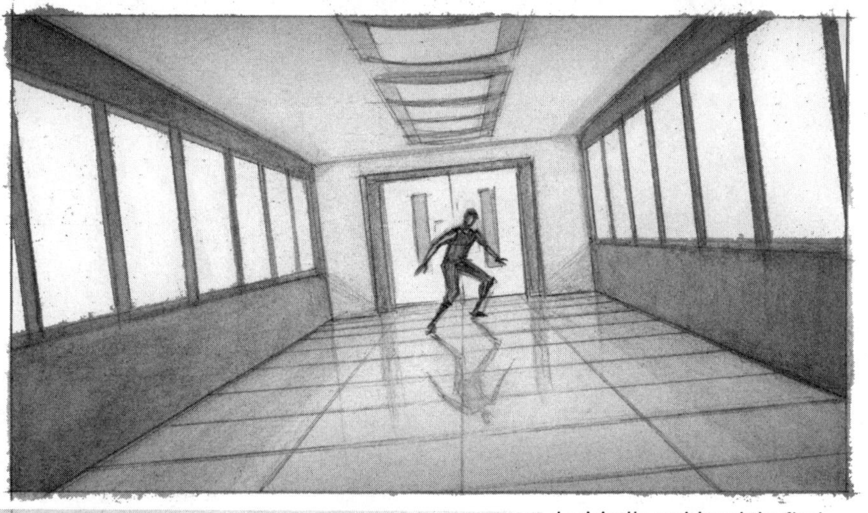

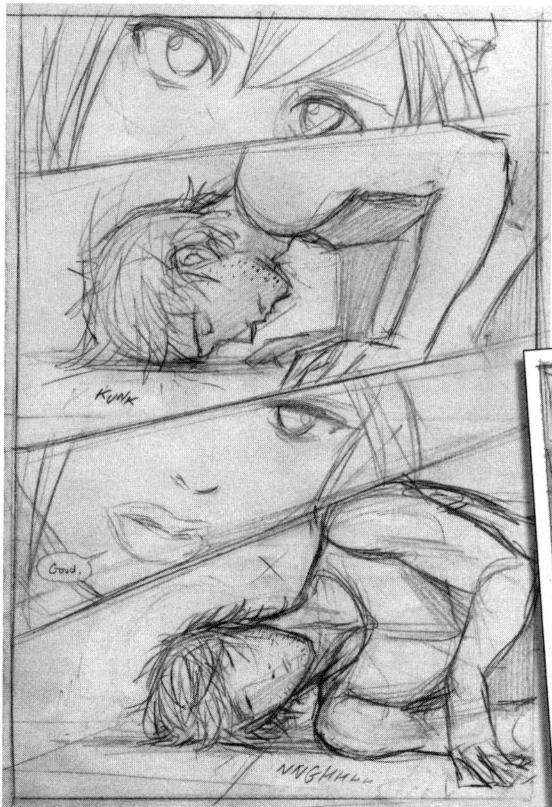
KUNK
Good.
NNGHHLL

I originally envisioned the final scene's skyway as a standard boxy space, but found that curving the walls made it less room-like and more tunnel-like.

In my first draft, one of the last pages would have included a panel of Brody losing consciousness in the skyway. I later chose to focus exclusively on him struggling to keep his head from hitting the floor, and to leave the moment of his final collapse to the reader's imagination.

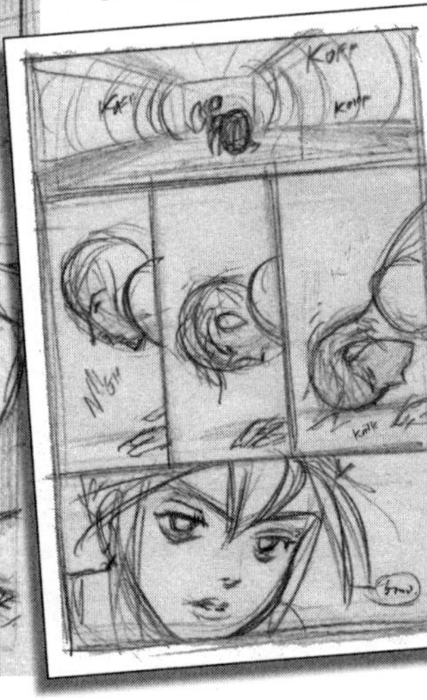

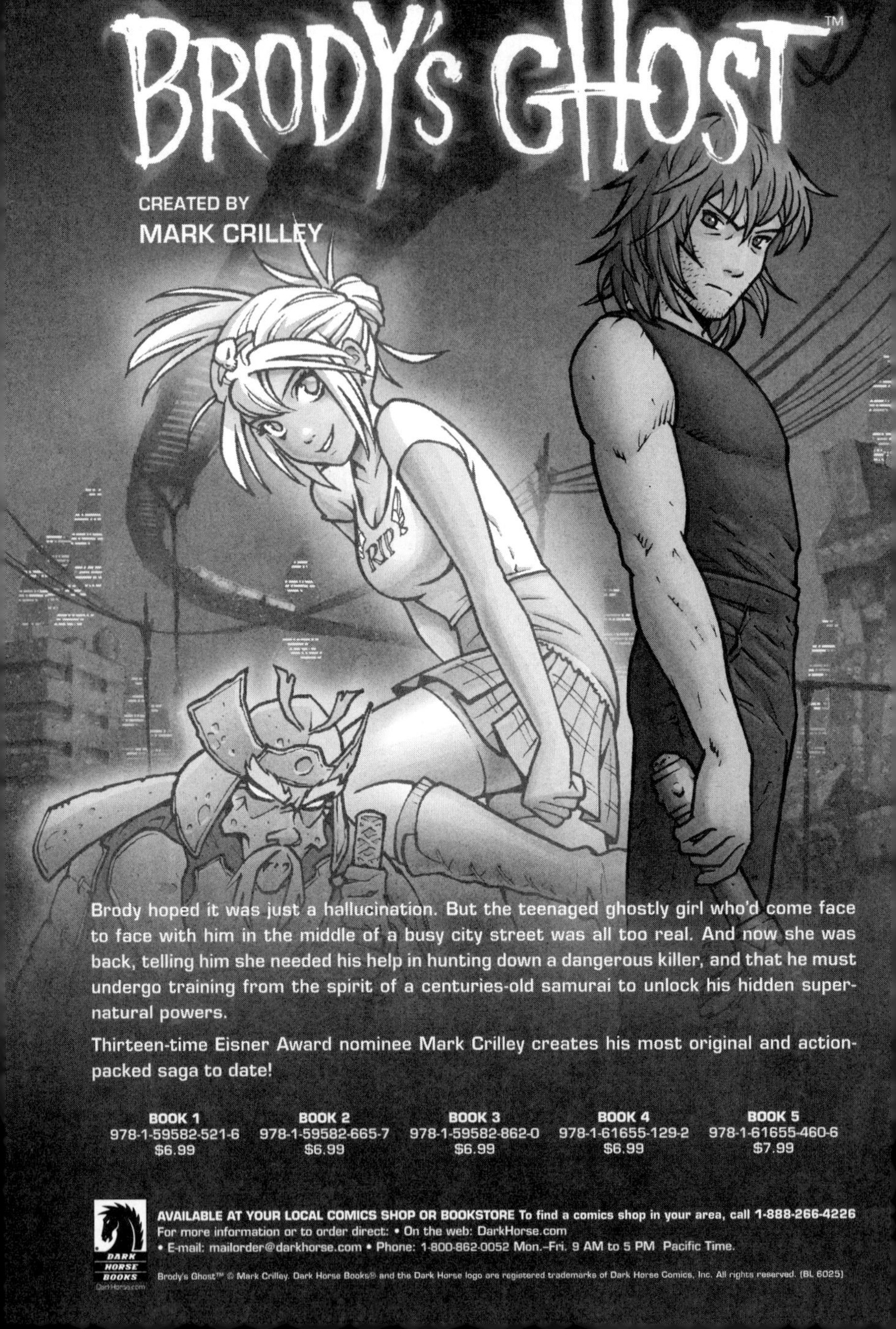
BRODY'S GHOST™
CREATED BY
MARK CRILLEY
RIP

Brody hoped it was just a hallucination. But the teenaged ghostly girl who'd come face to face with him in the middle of a busy city street was all too real. And now she was back, telling him she needed his help in hunting down a dangerous killer, and that he must undergo training from the spirit of a centuries-old samurai to unlock his hidden super-natural powers.

Thirteen-time Eisner Award nominee Mark Crilley creates his most original and action-packed saga to date!

BOOK 1	BOOK 2	BOOK 3	BOOK 4	BOOK 5
978-1-59582-521-6	978-1-59582-665-7	978-1-59582-862-0	978-1-61655-129-2	978-1-61655-460-6
$6.99	$6.99	$6.99	$6.99	$7.99

DARK HORSE BOOKS
DarkHorse.com

AVAILABLE AT YOUR LOCAL COMICS SHOP OR BOOKSTORE To find a comics shop in your area, call 1-888-266-4226
For more information or to order direct: • On the web: DarkHorse.com
• E-mail: mailorder@darkhorse.com • Phone: 1-800-862-0052 Mon.–Fri. 9 AM to 5 PM Pacific Time.